Sir
Winston Churchill:

Sir Winston Churchill: His Life and Times

MAXWELL P. SCHOENFELD
Wisconsin State University, Eau Claire

The Dryden Press
901 North Elm Street
Hinsdale, Illinois 60521

To Dick and Judie and Sarah Beth

Copyright © 1973 by The Dryden Press
All Rights Reserved
Library of Congress Catalog Card Number: 72-93889
ISBN: 0-03-086722-3
Printed in the United States of America
2345-090-987654321

Preface

The life of Sir Winston Churchill spans a remarkable period of human history. He was born well before the development of the automobile and the airplane, and personally participated in one of the last great cavalry charges in history. He was in middle age before the advent of the radio, and the first jet aircraft flew as he approached his seventieth birthday. Churchill was still active in politics into the age of the intercontinental ballistic missile and the hydrogen bomb. Sir Winston's public career touched almost every significant political development of the first half of the twentieth century. It included the coming of social democracy and the welfare state to Europe, the closing out of colonialism in Asia and Africa, two world wars, and the rise to world power of the United States and the Soviet Union. His life is virtually a personal history of man's fate in an era extraordinary alike for its splendid opportunities and its terrifying dangers.

If there is any theme to Sir Winston Churchill's life, it is surely his belief, upon which he vigorously acted, that man's destiny is unique, and that he is more than a speck of life, tossed upon the waves of chaos and swept along by the current of forces beyond his comprehension and control. Churchill's life was a monumental personal struggle to participate in his own fate and the shaping of his own destiny; that is the story I have tried to tell here. This is only one account among many of a man and of a time which still confront our own age with questions of interpretation and evaluation that are far from being resolved. Hopefully the reader of this brief account will find raised here issues significant enough to our own time that he will want to pursue them further, in the conviction that without knowledge and understanding of the past, we cannot find meaning in the present, or hope to see our way clear to the future.

Miss Kathleen Siedenburg and Mr. Larry Steen both did great service at a critical time in translating my illegible hand into an intelligible typescript. Mrs. Sue Gambrell skillfully prepared the finished version. My good friend and colleague, Professor Robert S. Fraser, read every word of this account, which gained much from his careful criticism and thoughtful suggestions. Its defects are, of course, entirely my own.

Eau Claire, Wisconsin   M. P. S.
August, 1971

Contents

Sir
Winston Churchill:
His Life and Times

CHAPTER ONE

Child of the Victorian Age: 1874—1900

Winston Leonard Spencer Churchill was born at Blenheim Palace on November 30, 1874, the first child of Lord Randolph Churchill and his American wife, the former Jennie Jerome. Young Winston was born into the British aristocracy in an era that honored social status and ancient title as much as it did great wealth, and young Winston had some claim to both. His mother came from well-to-do New York society while his father was a younger son of the Duke of Marlborough. But Winston's future was not assured by this alone; the English aristocracy still passed on to the eldest son not just their title of nobility but also the substantial funds and broad acres expected to support such dignity. Thus, Winston's father bore the title of Lord by courtesy only; as a younger son, he was expected to make his own way in the world. His lot, to be sure, was better beyond comparison than that of the average English working man or European peasant of the 1870s. Family, education and associations combined to offer him opportunities available only to the few. Yet opportunity had to be grasped; achievement required ability and ambition. Lord Randolph had both; his son would eclipse him in each.

It was not intended that Winston would be born in the great stone monument erected in Oxfordshire to the memory of the first Duke of Marlborough, one of the greatest of English military commanders. Blenheim Palace, named after the greatest of the victories of a man who fought ten major campaigns and nearly a hundred actions, great and small, without a defeat, had been completed by his termagant widow, Sarah, only with difficulty and amid growing recriminations. Appropriately, the Churchill family motto was "Faithful but Unfortunate." The premature child delivered by Lady Randolph would, like his father, live by that motto for most of his life.

Winston's grandfather, the seventh Duke of Marlborough, had inherited from his spendthrift predecessors Blenheim Palace and an encumbered estate to support its ageing grandeur. He had lived quietly and done duty in Tory politics under the great Conservative Prime Minister and favorite of Queen Victoria, Benjamin Disraeli. Lord Randolph had followed his father into politics, but more actively. He had been elected to the House of Commons from the old family seat of Woodstock only nine months before Winston's birth. Already he had attracted notice in Parliament, and put himself forward earlier than was customary or even thought proper in young members. But Lord Randolph was not much inhibited by such proprieties; his son would show a similar independence and ambition in his behavior. Nothing in Lady Randolph's family would add restraint; her father had made and lost several fortunes in the United States, a country whose energetic capitalist class caused the European aristocracy both shock and envy. The beautiful Jennie Jerome, vigorous and headstrong, was her father's daughter in all this. The attraction between Winston's parents had been nearly immediate upon their meeting. The courtship was short by the standards of their era and class; the two strong-willed lovers had not been deterred by counsels of caution from both families. Their marriage took place in the British Embassy in Paris on April 15, 1874. Interestingly, this building had been purchased by the Duke of Wellington when that great soldier had come to Paris in triumph sixty years earlier.

Thus the shades of England's two greatest soldiers seemed to preside over the beginnings of the career of England's greatest war minister.

The Duke of Wellington's victory over Napoleon Bonaparte at Waterloo in 1815 had seemed to ratify Britain's claim to preeminence among the powers of the world. The Iron Duke's victory ushered in an era of European peace and prosperity for those well placed in society. The Royal Navy, greater than its next several rivals combined, and inspired by the reputation of Horatio Nelson, guarded Britain's world-wide Empire and secured what was called in comparison to a more ancient empire, the "Pax Britannica." Prosperity had broadened down in Britain in the years before and after Waterloo from landed aristocracy to commercial and manufacturing classes. The soldier who had stood successfully against Napoleon in the field had become the politician who had yielded reluctantly to Earl Grey and the Whigs in Parliament in their demands for a reformed representation and franchise extended to the respectable British middle class in 1832. Although there were hard times in England in the late 1830s and 1840s, and terrible starvation in Ireland, the middle years of the nineteenth century saw Britain advance in wealth and its society in manners. In 1837, the woman who gave her name to this process and this era became Queen Victoria. Wealth flowed in from the British Empire, and the bloody events of a rising in India in the 1850s gave way in memory to Disraeli's proclamation of Victoria as Empress of that subcontinent in 1876. Already, that same shrewd Conservative politician had extended the franchise to urban householders in Britain in 1867, in the hope of beating his Liberal rival, William E. Gladstone, some critics said. If so, Disraeli's victory was postponed until 1874, for elections on the new franchise had given Gladstone a majority in 1868 and marked the beginning of a brilliant ministry that would end only shortly before Winston's birth.

In retrospect, the new franchise and the new ministry seemed to mark the beginning of a new time of broader participation in political life and a rising public expectation of the role government would play in their affairs. An education act in 1870 had gone a long way toward establishing a national minimum standard of elementary education for every child. (This education did not become free until 1891.) Trade unions gained legal standing in 1871. Elections were safeguarded by the secret ballot in an act of 1872. Entry into the civil service by competitive examination had become general, except for the foreign service, in 1870. Even the army, traditional home of aristocratic privilege, had yielded to reform in 1871. Promotion became open to ability, without the old requirement of purchase which had helped produce the aristocratic incompetents of the Crimean War. What was then considered a short active service of six years had already replaced the old twelve year active enlistment. Regiments had been given territorial districts as a basis for recruitment, and were organized into linked battalions, one serving at home while the other was abroad on imperial duty. These reforms of Edward Cardwell, Gladstone's War Secretary, gave the shape to the army into which Winston Churchill would pass in 1895, elements of which he could still recognize when he laid down his offices of Prime Minister and Minister of Defense in 1945.

Lord Randolph Churchill's election to Parliament in 1874 had been part of a Tory victory that had turned out Gladstone and returned the ageing Disraeli to power. In 1876 the elder statesman accepted a peerage as Earl of Beaconsfield. In his youth, he had described England as two nations, the privileged and the poor; in power he had sought to rival Gladstone in reforms designed to better the lot of the less fortunate nation. But Disraeli's concern for the welfare of the English masses was matched by his concern to preserve the traditional institutions of aristocratic privilege and thus, inevitably, aristocratic power. At the root of Disraeli's politics therefore lay a basic incompatibility which political skill and polished rhetoric could cover but not resolve. Lord Randolph Churchill would in his day take up Disraeli's politics with an audacity that equalled the old master's, but not with an equal skill. It was a tradition that would be passed on to Lord Randolph's son even into an era when democracy was triumphing over the institutions of aristocratic privilege.

It has been wisely said that every age is an age of transition, but the two decades of Winston's youth and of his father's political career were more so than most. For Britain's wealth and power, and her vast Empire, rested upon circumstances that were changing dramatically in the last third of the nineteenth century. Britain had led her European rivals in mating an efficient system for the amassing of capital with an efficient system for the mass production of manufactured goods. Her island geography had both protected her from invasion and had made easy the development of a coherent central government, which still-divided Germans and Italians might envy at the time of the Great Exhibition of 1851, when proud Britain had displayed her wares to the world. Europe led the world in the arts of government, economics, technology, and manufacture—and Britain led Europe. European dominion over subject peoples, a few thousand British ruling many millions of Indians, rested upon these advantages of organization and military technology, exploited with audacity—and indeed, not without ruthlessness. But such advantages were not permanent, neither England's advantage over her European rivals, nor Europe's privileged place among the continents. By the birth of Winston Churchill, both had begun to wear away. Germany had been united by blood and iron by 1871, and Italian unity was completed in the same year. These two new nations would compete with the older European states to carve up Africa even as German and American industry would strive to eclipse British manufacturers in the markets of the world.

But problems had not come only from foreign rivals; there was unrest inside the British Empire also. In particular, the oldest province of that Empire, Ireland, was proving hardest to rule. Pitt the Younger had attempted to solve this difficulty by incorporating Ireland into the United Kingdom in 1800 by an Act of Union. At first, this had brought the representatives of the Protestant Anglo-Irish Ascendancy class to the Imperial Parliament at Westminster as members, but in the 1820s Daniel O'Connell led native Catholic Irish into Parliament, where they forcefully pressed their demands. Gladstone had passed a land act in 1870 designed to protect the rural tenant; it was one among many Irish acts. But Irish expectations had risen, too. In Parliament there had appeared Charles Stewart Parnell, Protestant but passionately patriotic Irishman, who was prepared to disrupt the functioning of Parliament itself in order to secure Home Rule for Ireland.

It was not these harsh realities in Ireland that Winston remembered from his youth. He had gone as a child to Dublin when his grandfather had been Viceroy there. He could remember his mother, beautiful but distant, returning from the hunt. Like most children of his age and class, young Winston was entrusted to the care of a nanny, a Mrs. Everest, whose devotion to Winston and his younger brother, Jack, was reciprocated by them. But this happy beginning had to yield to the requirements of education when Winston was only eight, and his first experience was unhappy. Winston's first schooling has been called "one long feud with authority." For Winston was growing up a lonely, stubbornly independent boy who got little sympathetic understanding from his parents or anyone else, so he increasingly took refuge in his romantic imagination which would grow into a powerful instrument over time. Young Winston's mind was strong and retentive, and his education was somewhat happier after he entered the famous old English "Public" School of Harrow in 1888. Yet by that date his family had sustained calamitous misfortune; his father's career was ruined.

Lord Randolph had been a young man in a hurry. The ranks of the Conservative Party were crowded with experienced politicians with claims upon office when he entered Parliament in 1874. As Parnell's Irish made a third party to the traditional Tories and Liberals, Lord Randolph and some friends called themselves the "fourth party" and acted to draw the attention of the Tory leadership to themselves. Lord Randolph was a powerful speaker, was ready to appeal to the British democracy with policies designed to attract votes, and would try to negotiate terms with Parnell. The Tories needed much vigor with Disraeli ageing—he died in 1881. So Lord Randolph rose rapidly in the Conservative Party. Gladstone had returned to office in 1880 and had decided finally for Irish Home Rule at the end of 1885. Gladstone's Home Rule proposal split the Liberal Party, with Lord Hartington and Joseph Chamberlain leading supporters of the Irish Union over to the Tories in 1886.

The election of that year was a Conservative and Unionist triumph that made Lord Salisbury Prime Minister, and Lord Randolph Churchill Chancellor of the Exchequer and Leader of the House of Commons. It was a brilliant achievement for a young man. But between the Prime Minister and his Leader of the House of Commons lay a gulf of attitude and outlook which threatened to divide the Tories as the Liberals had been split. Lord Randolph leaned toward reform at home and financial retrenchment in the military operations that policed Britain's Empire abroad; Lord Salisbury distrusted his ambitious lieutenant as much as he distrusted the good judgment of the British masses. When Lord Randolph resigned the Chancellorship, thinking thus to force Salisbury to accept his financial policy to keep him, Salisbury accepted the resignation. For Salisbury did not need him: others could serve as the Prime

Minister's links with the masses whose votes he needed, and another man could be found to run the Treasury.

Lord Randolph had cast away his career; he was ruined. His fate fell as a dark shadow upon young Winston, who had followed his father's career avidly even as he was unable to approach his temperamentally difficult father, who neglected his elder son and appeared to have thought little of him. It is perhaps hard to criticize Lord Randolph for after 1886 he was a sick man, and would die in public by inches. It was a cruel ordeal for the whole family, and left its mark upon the sensitive Winston.

England was changing even as young Winston was growing up. In that dramatic political year of 1886 a philanthropic shipowner, Charles Booth, initiated a study of London poverty that would eventually conclude that 30% of the population of that great metropolis lived below a less-than-generous poverty line. In some "sweated" trades, the employees, especially women, labored in truly grim conditions. B. Seebohm Rowntree found that 43% of York's working population lacked an income adequate to sustain bare physical needs. Booth was moved to describe thousands of Londoners "seeking their livelihood under conditions . . . on the middle ground between civilization and barbarism." He observed a typical street inhabited by the poor:

> . . . just wide enough for a vehicle to pass either way, with room between curb-stone and houses for one foot-passenger to walk; but vehicles would pass seldom, and foot-passengers would prefer the roadway to the risk of tearing their clothes against projecting nails. . . . In little rooms no more than 8 ft. square, would be found living father, mother, and several children. . . . Drunkenness and dirt and bad language prevailed, and violence was common, reaching at times even to murder. Fifteen rooms out of twenty were filthy to the last degree. . . . Not a room would be free from vermin, and in many life at night was unbearable. Several occupants have said that in hot weather they don't go to bed, but sit in their clothes in the least infested part of the room. What good is it, they said, to go to bed when you can't get a wink of sleep for bugs and fleas? A visitor in these rooms was fortunate indeed if he carried nothing of the kind away with him. . . . The little yard at the back was only sufficient for dust-bin and closet and water-tap, serving for six or seven fami-

lies. The water would be drawn from cisterns which were receptacles for refuse, and perhaps occasionally a dead cat.[1]

Not surprisingly, the poor sought escape from such living conditions in the numerous local pubs, and Rowntree noted that "their social attractiveness struck him very forcibly." He felt strongly "the need for the establishment on Temperance lines of something equally attractive in this respect." His concern was widely shared, for public drunkenness was a serious social problem in Britain before World War I. Rowntree observed at one pub: "Between 5 and 6 P.M. a woman was ejected. A row immediately ensued, the woman using language unfit for human ears. As usual, a crowd of children were keenly enjoying the scene, which lasted for about three-quarters of an hour."[2]

Rowntree also fairly noted that there was in the pubs "an air of jollity and an absence of irksome restraint which must prove very attractive after a day's confinement in factory or shop." But even for the most sober and industrious poor the outlook was dim. Rowntree gave a typical example:

This household consists of a father, aged 37, mother 35, and three girls aged 8, 6, and 2½ years. Mr. S. is a very steady worker. This is a fairly typical home of the labouring class, though on the whole it is much neater than the average. The 'missus' is manager, and a very careful one, and well supported by the husband, who indulges in no unnecessary luxuries. They are members of the Co-operative Stores, and buy in their groceries at the end of each week, and take care that every penny is well spent. . . . The children are well looked after. . . . An examination of this family's diet shows that the protein is 29 per cent and the fuel value is 25 per cent below standard requirements.[3]

Rowntree concluded that the chief cause of poverty was that "wages paid for unskilled labour . . . are insufficient to provide food, shelter, and clothing adequate to maintain a family of moderate size in a state of bare physical efficiency."[4]

Such conditions contrasted harshly with grand visions of a wealthy, imperial Britain, and it attracted critics. Earlier, British capitalism had been harshly portrayed by Frederich Engels, and in 1884 an avowedly Marxist Social Democratic Federation had been formed in England, although without Marx's support. Less radical and more practical was the Fabian Society, whose reformist enterprises were led forward slowly but surely by Sidney and Beatrice Webb, pioneering social historians. The Fabian Society brought social reformers into contact with politicians. Indeed, sensitive politicians were aware of the unrest stirring amid poverty. In 1894, the Liberal Chancellor, Harcourt, adopted a proposal of Lord Randolph Churchill's of graduated death duties upon personal and real property alike. Such a policy, consciously applied or not, meant nothing less than a redistribution of wealth by government action. This was a profound departure from the canons of orthodox nineteenth century Liberalism, which had conceived of the State as safeguarding man's economic opportunities but not regulating man's economic behavior. But Lord Salisbury and the Conservatives dominated the two decades, 1886-1906. The Liberal Gladstone's last Home Rule bill was defeated in 1893, and Salisbury returned to office in the elections of 1895. That election had been disastrous to working-class aspirations. Harcourt had been defeated, as had been most radically inclined candidates. None of the candidates of the new Independent Labour Party was successful. Lord Randolph was gone and the gap between Disraeli's two nations remained unbridged.

Young Winston lived among the privileged section. At Harrow he demonstrated his tenacious memory in winning a prize for reciting without error 1,200 lines of poetry. But his aptitude did not impress his father, and he was indeed an erratic and unruly scholar. Lord Randolph decided Winston should prepare for the army—not a compliment to his son—and Winston was put into the Army Class at Harrow in 1889. As Winston's mathematics were weak, artillery and engineering were ruled out; as he was recklessly bold, the infantry and cavalry—especially the latter—seemed suitable. The British cavalry were notable for their bravery and their general uselessness alike; this reputation stayed with them from the days when Wellington had cursed his cavalry in the Peninsula, right down to the Charge of the Light Brigade in the Crimean War. But the expenses of a cavalry cadet at Sandhurst—the military academy—were high, and the Churchill family finances low, and so Lord Randolph hoped Winston's examination scores would be high enough to command an infantry cadetship.

But Winston's examination scores on the first try in 1892 were not enough even to get him in. On the second try he was still short, but tutoring led to a cavalry cadetship in June of 1893 on the third try at the examinations. Lord Randolph was not impressed by his son's performance, and when a happy Winston wrote him news of success at last, he replied in a long and crushing letter. His son was berated for repeated "folly and failure." With this blessing from his ill parent, Winston entered the Royal Military College at Sandhurst shortly before his nineteenth birthday. For nearly another year his father's fatal condition was kept from him, and only in 1894 did the family physician inform Winston that his father would return from a world tour more dead than alive. Final paralysis carried off Lord Randolph on January 24, 1895 and he was put to rest in Bladon churchyard within sight of Blenheim Palace. Seventy years later, Lord Randolph's son would follow him in death and finally to rest in the same churchyard.

Winston was just past twenty. His mother was extravagant as ever and could offer him no financial support. Winston would have to make his own career. He did well at Sandhurst and passed out 20th in a class of 130, and he entered the 4th Hussars, a well commanded cavalry regiment, in February, 1895. He swore his oath to Queen Victoria, the first of six sovereigns he would serve. As a young officer he was not too busy, or too poor, to try to aid his old nanny, Mrs. Everest, who died in the summer of 1895. But even as England was changing, so was Winston, and his ties to the past were now few. Winston realized he had his own way to make in the world. At much the same time he realized how important a good education was to his future, and how erratic his own studies had been. So the young cavalry officer embarked upon a program of self-learning even as he labored to master his profession. He was never to lack for either ambition or energy.

To Winston, the practice of a professional soldier required a war, and there was none available on the frontiers of the British Empire in 1895. There was, however, a difficult struggle in Cuba between native forces and the ruling Spanish. Churchill decided to visit the action, and his mother's native land on the way. Taking a rather generous view of his leave from the army, Winston contracted with a London newspaper to write back letters from Cuba. His practice of recording his experiences, and earning a needed income from his writing, would be carried on throughout his life, culminating in his monumental memoirs of World War II. Winston reached the United States late in 1895 and sent back his first impressions to his brother Jack of that nation, which was to be so important in Churchill's future and the world's affairs in time to come. He called the United States a "very great country," a land not pretty or romantic but great and utilitarian, and without much reverence for tradition. He was, however, shocked by the restrictiveness of West Point, compared to the independence and respect for individuality allowed at Sandhurst.

In Cuba, he managed to come under fire and to earn some money from five newspaper articles. Perhaps most important, he had succeeded in attracting attention to himself, and upon returning to London he cultivated the company of the powerful on the basis of his family name and his recent experiences. It seems this early Winston was thinking beyond the army toward the day when he would take up the political career his father had tragically left off. By August of 1896 he had made his ambition explicit to his mother: he sought a military reputation which would win his way into Parliament. Thus he was impatient for action.

He did not at once get it. His regiment was sent to India, quiet at that moment. He sailed East filled with ambition, like many Englishmen before him, but also with frustration, for he believed it was taking him farther from, not nearer to, his political goal. But he did not waste his time; he labored to correct a speech impediment, which indeed was always noticeable throughout his life. Opinion has differed on the exact nature of Winston's impediment; some who heard him speak believed it was a stammer; others called it a lisp. He always had trouble pronouncing the letter S, as had Lord Randolph. A doctor who examined Winston declared that the speech impediment was not caused by any organic defect, which leads to speculation regarding the psychological impact of Lord Randolph upon his sensitive son, Winston.

The land he sailed toward was viewed as the brightest jewel of the British Empire, and India embodied both the aspirations and problems of that Empire at the end of the nineteenth century. By 1896, the British justification for holding India had come to rest upon what Britain could do for the welfare of the Indian people, not what material gains might flow to the British from this imperial possession. Lord Salisbury, the Prime Minister, held this view, and Winston Churchill was to hold it throughout his life. Without any sense of incongruity, one British official could refer to "the magnificent work of governing an inferior race." It was admitted that British control of India rested not upon consent, but upon conquest; to be both legitimate and durable, that control must. be exercised in the best interests of the ruled. As late as 1896 many Englishmen could believe with confidence they were doing this; yet in that same year British tariff legislation tied Indian trade more tightly to Britain, and was resented in India. Further, the ultimate standard of the well-being of peoples by British standards was self-government by the forms of parliamentary democracy. The white settlement colonies, like Canada and Australia, were well along that road. Was the same standard to apply to India? This seemed very much a hypothetical question to an Englishman in 1896. Indians seemed hopelessly far from governing themselves by the standards he recognized as fitting. But who was the proper judge of this: Englishman or Indian?

India posed not only a dilemma of constitutional and moral principle for the English imperialist, it also posed a problem of international power politics. As nations like Germany and the United States rose to rival the preeminence of Britain, the more obvious became Britain's dependence upon her Empire for her place in the world, and the more vulnerable that Empire appeared to the ambitions of possible foes. Some Englishmen had long feared Russian ambitions both toward India and toward the long line of communications that ran out from Britain, through the Mediterranean and Suez, down the Red Sea and across the Indian Ocean. And if Russia seemed to threaten the Suez lifeline from one direction, there was a potential French threat across North Africa toward Egypt and the Sudan from the other direction. And what were Italy's ambitions in the Mediterranean? The more vulnerable the lifeline appeared, the more important it was to safeguard it by strong positions on the Persian Gulf and southern Arabia, in Egypt and the Sudan and on the Mediterranean. But each of these in turn threatened to become a "vital interest" to Britain. Where did Britain's interest leave off? And was Britain, dwelling in "splendid isolation," capable of defending what were believed to be her interests? It is easy in retrospect to understand why that somber realist, Lord Salisbury, presided over this Empire from London without hope for the future, and indeed, with limited confidence in the present. The circumstances that had permitted the accumulation of the British Empire were disappearing even as Englishmen celebrated its apogee in the Jubilee observances of Victoria's reign in 1887 and 1897.

Something of this was already grasped by the young man of twenty-two who sailed for India. He wrote his mother that it was foolish for Parliament to be proposing to increase the British Army; the army was large enough to garrison the Empire already but could hardly be expanded to rival the size of European conscript armies. It should be a defensive force only. In this remarkable letter, Churchill went on to spell out his political ideas at this time. He called himself a Tory democrat and advocated a full adult male franchise and universal education. He wanted domestic reform, an eight-hour working day, and payment of Members of Parliament, which would enable working class members to sit. He favored a progressive income tax. He wished to stay out of European politics entirely. But he advocated also maintaining the Empire, and evidently did not see that the price of this might have to be alliance with some European powers. Nor did he believe that democratic government was possible east of Suez, and he had not even seen India yet. A great navy and small army would furnish imperial defense. Winston's attitudes toward domestic politics placed him among progressives at home. But like most Englishmen he seemed as yet not fully conscious that Britain's Empire would require facing hard choices; the options of policy open in world affairs were narrowing dramatically at the end of the nineteenth century. Empire would carry a high price-tag. A famous demagogue once cried out the question: What ransom would the British wealthy pay for the security of their property? Perhaps he should have asked what ransom would Britain pay for its Empire. Perhaps it was to be the blood-ransom of the Somme and Passchendaele during World War I.

When he sailed to India, Churchill was mercifully unaware of these future horrors he would have some day to confront. Diligently he prepared for his political career, dutifully laboring through 27 volumes of the *Annual Register*, that encyclopedia of recent British and world politics, economics, and statistics. Churchill would always display a desire to support his political positions with heavy documentation and weighty evidence; it was an early passion with him. He read also the histories of Edward Gibbon and Lord Macaulay, and these would influence his literary style.

Once in India, he found ways to get assigned to a frontier expedition. He wrote his mother that such frontier service would increase his claims to be listened to, and improve his prospects for political popularity at home. But he was not just a coldblooded adventurer. He admitted that he enjoyed running risks; he never lost his taste for the dangerous. Life was always exciting for Churchill and the world he lived in was always a romantic place. He got his action in the Malakand frontier region and displayed the courage under fire which was also a life-long characteristic. Again he reported the action for a newspaper and soon embarked upon his first published book, an account of the Malakand Field Force. It brought him the money and public notice he needed for a political career. He was ready to return from India, for by 1898, public attention was turning from Asia toward Africa.

When Disraeli bought an interest in the Suez Canal in 1875, Britain became enmeshed in the affairs of Egypt. Disorders there had brought a British occupation in 1882. An interest in Egypt meant an interest in the entire Nile River basin which was the strategic backbone and economic lifeblood of Egypt. The British occupation of Egypt was a part of a late surge, almost a frenzy, of European imperialism. The African continent, largely left to its inhabitants as late as 1870, was, with the notable exceptions of Ethiopia and Liberia, to be largely parcelled out among the European powers by 1900. To gain a free hand in Egypt, Britain had abandoned most of Equatorial Africa to French ambition. But the Sudan, the region on the Nile above Egypt, remained an indeterminent zone. In 1885, General Charles Gordon had paid for his recklessness with his life when the forces of a regional fanatic, the Mahdi, had overrun Khartoum and massacred every Englishman there, a disaster that had shaken the government of that most reluctant of all imperialists, William E. Gladstone, who refused further involvement during his ministry.

Not till 1896 did a British conquest of this area begin in earnest; it was by an Anglo-Egyptian army commanded by Sir Herbert Kitchener, a formidable soldier of British imperialism. By 1898 his slow advance toward Khartoum and revenge for Gordon's fate was about to be achieved. Winston Churchill wished to be there. Kitchener deeply disapproved of Churchill's exploitation of military service for political popularity and refused to have him. Churchill's ambition did not stop him from seeking the aid of Lord Salisbury, the man who had destroyed his father, but it was the Adjutant-General of the British Army, Sir Evelyn Wood, who appointed Churchill an extra officer to the 21st Lancers, a British cavalry regiment in Kitchener's forces. Churchill left hurriedly for Cairo, after first contracting with the *Morning Post* for his dispatches from the front. He was just in time for the action, joining the regiment only a few miles short of Khartoum. Two goals lay there for British forces; avenging Gordon was only the first. By 1898 ambitious British imperialists like Cecil Rhodes dreamed of a British Empire in Africa which would run from Cairo to Capetown. Control of the Sudan was an essential step in this. France also had African visions, of a French Africa stretching from French Northwest Africa and Lake Chad in the west toward French Somaliland on the Red Sea. The Sudan lay across this vision; there was not room for Englishmen and Frenchmen both on the upper Nile. Kitchener meant to be in physical possession before the French arrived.

What the young Churchill saw was not only these power politics but the bustle of Cairo bazaars, the muddy reddish-brown of the life-giving Nile, the sand-grey of desert barren of life which captured his romantic nature as it had Englishmen before him and would Englishmen after him. His own vision would turn to the Middle East again and again, in World War I and World War II. The most graphic book he would ever write was *The River War,* his account of Kitchener's Nile River campaign. The climax of that campaign came at Omdurman on September 2, 1898. There, along the Nile riverbank, the wild dervishes of the Sudan attacked and broke themselves against the disciplined fire-power of Kitchener's Anglo-Egyptian forces. Late in the battle the British cavalry had attacked the dervishes, one of the last great cavalry charges in history. It was set down from experience by Churchill in one of the last great accounts of the horrible grandeur of war:

> I had first of all to return my sword into its scabbard, which is not the easiest thing to do at a gallop. I had then to draw my pistol from its wooden holster and bring it to full cock. . . . Then I saw immediately before me . . . the row of crouching blue figures firing frantically. . . . The collision was now very near. I saw immediately before me . . . two blue men who lay in my path. . . . I rode at the interval between them. They both fired. I passed through the smoke conscious that I was unhurt. The trooper immediately behind me was killed. . . . Suddenly in the midst of the troop up sprang a Dervish. . . . Wounded several times, he staggered towards me raising his spear. I shot him at less than a yard. . . . But now from the direction of the enemy there came . . . men bleeding from terrible wounds, fish-hook spears stuck right through them, arms and faces

cut to pieces, bowels protruding. . . . Out of 310 officers and men
the regiment had lost in the space of two or three minutes five
officers and sixty-five men killed and wounded. . . . [5]

Soon, even for the romantic Churchill, only horror without grandeur
would remain to war. He would face later danger with the same unflinching courage he displayed in the charge at Omdurman, but never
again with the same feelings. After the battle he felt for the terribly
defeated dervishes a compassion he always would extend to a conquered foe. Churchill's compassion withstood all the shocks of battle
and bruises of politics alike to make him one of the most humane of
statesmen. In his long life he suffered at first-hand all the repeated
misfortunes which twentieth-century man inflicted upon himself without losing hope for mankind. Churchill's greatness lay in his simple but
strong humanity.

Kitchener was concerned with reaping the harvest of victory. To
Churchill's rage, Khartoum was occupied and the Mahdi's Tomb de-
filed. Kitchener proceeded on up the Nile to Fashoda, which a French
expedition had already reached. The French were ordered out. They
refused to go. Appeal for a decision was made to the home governments. The loss of Alsace and Lorraine to Germany in 1871 meant
more to the French Foreign Minister than loss of the Sudan to Britain
in 1898. He wanted British friendship against the day of reckoning with
his German foe; the French withdrew from Fashoda.

At much the same time Churchill also made a critical decision; he
resigned his commission in the army and returned to England. He put
his hopes in profits from *The River War* and future writings; his aim was
Parliament. His first political campaign came in the summer of 1899
when he stood as one of the two Conservative candidates for the industrial constituency of Oldham in Lancashire. His chances were not good.
The Tory government was unpopular in the area at the time, and the
Liberals were running strong candidates. The poll on July 6 revealed
that Churchill had lost. It was an appropriate enough beginning to a
political career of six decades that would see many election defeats as
well as many victories. Determination in the face of adversity was a
virtue Churchill was given ample opportunity to practice throughout a
long life.

In September, 1899, the Boer War broke out and the *Morning Post*
again hired Winston as its war correspondent. Churchill sailed hastily

for South Africa, hoping the war would not be over before he arrived. He was not disappointed, though the British would soon have cause to wish the war were concluded. The Boer War was to end for many Englishmen the pleasant illusions of "splendid isolation."

Britain had been interested in South Africa from the days before the Suez Canal when African ports were way-stations to India. Interest in the South African hinterland came later, largely the result of commercial initiatives, and encountered every sort of difficulty: from native resistance, from German and Portugese rivals, but particularly from Dutch settlers called Boers. This pastoral people, long cut off from their cosmopolitan homeland, possessed a closed, patriarchal, narrowly fundamentalist society. Unhappy with the growing English settlement, the Boers had trekked inland from the coastal Cape Colony and Natal. They established the Transvaal Republic and what became the Orange Free State, and the British had acknowledged their possession in the 1850s. But in the 1860s diamonds were discovered in the border region between the Orange Free State and the Cape Colony. This region was soon annexed to the British colony. As the British prospered, the Boers suffered and Disraeli then annexed the bankrupt Transvaal. The Boers, relieved of native danger through British efforts, promptly rebelled and defeated the British in the Battle of Majuba Hill in 1881.

Gladstone, unwilling to prosecute a vigorous imperialism, negotiated a settlement that left to Britain only a vague sovereignty. When gold in great quantity was found in the Transvaal in 1886, it exercised a magnetic attraction on men such as Cecil Rhodes, who had made a fortune in diamonds, was willing to make another fortune in gold, and who ever dreamed of a vast British Empire in Africa. British policy since Majuba Hill suggested a desire to make the Boer republics into economic satellites; Rhodes' ambitions likely went a good bit beyond this. The Boer leadership steadfastly sought independence from any British control. But Rhodes had an issue; the gold mines had created a non-Boer majority in the Transvaal, who were without political rights although they paid 90% of the taxes. At the end of 1895 Rhodes attempted a coup, the Jameson Raid, which failed. Continuing difficulties ended in the Boer leader Paul Kruger issuing an ultimatum in October 1899, just beating the British one which had been urged by Alfred Milner, the British High Commissioner at the Cape, and Joseph Chamberlain, the radical imperialist who was Salisbury's Colonial Secretary. The Boer

War came because both sides wanted it to come. Both sides would have ample occasion to reflect upon the unwisdom of their wishes.

At first, Boer soldiers outnumbered British, but the Boers squandered away their advantage and initiative in long seiges of three British strongholds at Kimberley, Ladysmith, and Mafeking. That the Boers had thrown away their opportunity was not at first clear to either side; over-confident Britons were stunned by reports of their forces driven back and their garrisons invested. Serious military operations were put under way, and two experienced commanders, Lords Roberts and Kitchener, arrived in South Africa early in 1900. All three British strongholds were relieved, two early in the year and Mafeking in May. Even though the Boer army appeared beaten, the Boers refused to yield and took to guerrilla warfare late in 1900. The British responded by a slow but thorough sweeping of the countryside. Non-combatants were swept up into concentration camps, where gross mismanagement produced a 19% death-rate and political reaction at home. But the Boers were done, and an armistice in March, 1902 was followed by the Peace of Vereeniging in May. The terms granted a broad amnesty, provided an oath be taken to the King; English became the official language, but Boer Dutch remained an option. Funds were furnished to start the task of rebuilding ruined farms. Milner acted as an enlightened if tough administrator in restoring civil administration and pointing the two Boer regions toward early self-government.

It was not a very glorious victory that required 350,000 British troops to subdue about 60,000 Boers. Further, world opinion had run sharply against the British. Only the American government, with its own imperial problems arising out of the Spanish-American War, seemed very understanding. The German government seemed the most hostile. Irish-Americans and British Liberals alike could denounce bullying of the Boers by an overbearing British imperial government. Little notice was attracted by an even deeper problem, the relations between European—Boers and English alike—and the native Blacks.

Churchill had arrived in South Africa when the Boer initiative was still at high-tide. With characteristic boldness he had rushed to the front. In November of 1899 an armored train he was on was ambushed by the Boers. Although technically a non-combatant, Churchill had led the effort to free the train from ambush and was instrumental in the escape of the engine. But Churchill himself was taken prisoner. He had been working in the open under fire and was slightly wounded. The British who escaped quickly related his courageous performance and his accomplishment received much play in England. A yet more spectacular performance followed. Churchill was lodged in a made-over school used to hold British officer prisoners in Pretoria. He promptly organized a plan to escape, even as he bombarded the Boer authorities with demands that he should be released as a non-combatant. He did not wait to get the Boer government's response, but went over the prison wall and made his way out of Pretoria alone, some others being unable to join him. With incredible luck, Churchill found aid from an Englishman in the area and was smuggled out of the Transvaal by rail to the Portugese Delagoa Bay and then back to the British forces. He was now indeed famous, for his remarkable escape with a price on his head gave British newspapers some good news to offset Boer victories.

Churchill remained in South Africa to participate in the relief of Ladysmith and to enter Pretoria where he could assist in freeing his comrades who had not gotten away. It all made rich copy for the *Morning Post* and Churchill's reporting was read widely in England. He would later produce two books out of his South African experiences. In the *Morning Post* as the British tide of victory began to run in early 1900, Churchill had recommended generous peace terms for the Boers. His customary magnanimity produced sharp criticism at home, although the British government was to act in accord with Churchill's wishes. But Churchill had achieved in South Africa what he had sought there, and when he sailed for England on July 4, 1900, he was a famous man still short of his twenty-sixth birthday. The voters were not likely to reject him again.

The Unionist government of Lord Salisbury, deciding to capitalize upon the wave of British victories, held a general election in the autumn of 1900. Again Churchill stood as a government candidate for Oldham, and on October 2, 1900, he was returned to Parliament when Liberals in the two-member constituency split their tickets as a compliment to Churchill's valor in South Africa. There followed speaking tours in the British Isles and North America, for Winston needed money—Members of Parliament were not yet paid. His writing and speaking combined to produce enough revenue to support his new dignity. At twenty-six years of age, Winston Churchill entered the mother of Parliaments which he was to love and serve for the rest of his life.

Notes to Chapter I:

1 Charles Booth, *Life and Labour of the People in London,* Second Edition (Macmillan, New York, 1892), II, 46-47.

2 B. Seebohm Rowntree, *Poverty, A Study of Town Life,* New Edition, reprinted (Fertig, New York, 1971), pp. 369, 374.

3 *Ibid.,* p. 326.

4 *Ibid.,* p. 166.

5 W. S. Churchill, *My Early Life: A Roving Commission,* paperback edition (Scribners, New York, 1958), pp. 183-194.

CHAPTER TWO

The Rising Politician: 1900–1911

The Victorian Age had been for Britain a blend of progress and continuity. While Britain had led the world in
industrialization, it had not sustained the violent political shocks that had accompanied social and economic
change on the continent. The solid, proper queen who
died in 1901 had personified this British stability. The
new monarch, Edward VII, was a more flamboyant person, enjoyed beautiful women, good food, and the good
life. The change in monarchs seemed to match a change
in popular sentiment, a new readiness to enjoy the
pleasures of a life improved by the solid progress of the
preceding reign. Vast British investment abroad now
brought handsome returns to the well-off classes.

But the gilded, Edwardian surface to English society
in the new century overlaid more somber realities.
Britain was no longer the world's first industrial power.
By 1906 it had been passed by the United States in steel,

iron, and coal production, and by Germany in steel. Both nations led Britain in electrical and chemical development. The return on Britain's overseas investments masked a deficit in the trade of goods.

These hard economic facts did not yet affect the self-confidence of the British ruling class. Old habits died hard and the rightness of British preeminence in the world, and their own leadership in Britain, was accepted by most of the British ruling class as the normal order of things. At the top, the ancient house of Cecil which had provided servants to Tudor and Stuart monarchs served Victoria and Edward as well; Lord Salisbury in 1902 was succeeded as Prime Minister by his nephew, A. J. Balfour. Both were brilliant men, and the elder somberly, the younger man skeptically, viewed the state of the world with a deeper appreciation of reality than most of their compatriots. They defended the interests of Britain and their class with ability but without enthusiasm.

Even as Britain's share of the world's wealth was challenged from abroad, at home voices questioned the distribution of that wealth within British society. The ostentation of the Edwardian ruling class stuck out in contrast to the drab poverty of a thousand urban streets grimed with the coal soot of dark factories where the laboring classes put in long, dull hours at work. The state of these people had been surveyed by the Webbs in their *History of Trade Unionism* (1897). Their middle-class social conscience was shocked by the hardships of the laboring classes even while their practical intelligence sought social improvement. The Webbs were instrumental in founding the London School of Economics to promote serious economic study and reform alike. The Fabian Society and other middle-class socialist societies had, by the turn of century, started to move away from efforts at permeating the traditional parties with reformist views and toward direct alliance with the working classes themselves. This would become a fruitful union. Near the end of the nineteenth century Keir Hardie, a former miner, had been elected to Parliament. Where Hardie led, others were prepared to follow, and an Independent Labour Party had formed ready to advocate working class goals through direct working class membership in Parliament. A Labour Representation Committee, representing both trade unions and socialist societies, had run candidates in the 1900 general election, but with little success. From this slight beginning would grow the British Labour Party. Only a few of the traditionalist politicians, like Joseph Chamberlain, seemed to realize where these early stirrings could eventually lead.

The only thing Churchill shared with the few working-class members who appeared at Westminster when the new Parliament assembled in early 1901 was a concern for personal economic independence. Like them, he was not wealthy, and Members of Parliament (M.P.'s) were not paid until 1911. But he had made his own way successfully within the gilded circle of privilege. Although Oldham was a working-class constituency, the twenty-six-year-old Winston was almost totally uninformed about either the factory system or working-class life. The very drabness of such institutions and life would assure that they did not catch the romantic young man's first attention. He would have to learn their importance. Fortunately, Churchill was always willing to learn, and perhaps in learning he would also come to care. Certainly his emotional, humane nature would always incline him toward a deep commitment to any endeavor he took up. First Winston had to learn the ways of the House of Commons. He had already looked down in his youth from the visitors' gallery upon individuals standing to speak in that oblong chamber too small to seat all its members which is the House of Commons. He later would affirm that this size was an advantage, allowing a conversational speaking style and retaining a sense of personality even in a nearly empty chamber; while on great occasions, the crowd of members would underline and enhance the significance and seriousness of momentous decisions by the House. Similarly, Churchill believed that the arrangement of benches along the long walls, facing each other across the floor of the House, encouraged a clear-cut political position. Either you belonged to the majority who supplied His Majesty's Government, or you sat in the minority opposite, who were called appropriately, His Majesty's Opposition. In such a House, issues could be debated to a conclusion, and put to a vote, or division as it is called in the House of Commons. If a division is called, members leave their places in the House to enter the respective aye and nay lobbies. Then back in from the lobbies the members would stream in two lines past the tellers, counting for government and opposition. These tellers usally are the Party Whips, some of the men among whose responsibilities in their parties was to muster all available supporters in the divisions. The four tellers would then advance to the Speaker's chair to announce the result. The wigged Speaker, the mace representing the authority of the House on the table before him, the government front bench to his right, and the opposition front bench across the table from them, were all traditional parts of the ancient representative assembly that Churchill venerated.

The House of Commons as a corporate body was a jealous mistress toward its suitors. Many who entered it with high hopes never gained its respect, or affection. Churchill was to win both, to a degree that the House has seldom extended to any member, but only after a long and often stormy courtship. Churchill was not a fluent extempore speaker, and wisely prepared his first speech for the House with care. In that first speech, Winston followed one of the rising stars of the opposition, a young Welsh radical, David Lloyd George, who criticized aspects of the government's South African policy. This early the two greatest Prime Ministers of the twentieth century faced each other, Churchill rising to defend the government. It was a capable beginning, as Winston knew his topic at first hand, but was without the burning flamboyance that had characterized his father's style. Speaking easily in the House was for a long time difficult for Winston, and in April, 1904, he lost his line of thought and had to sit down abruptly; those with memories of his father's tragic decline feared a second such misfortune. But it was only a setback, and with experience, Churchill's rhetorical skill in the House grew.

His setback had arisen from the great trouble Winston had in speaking extemporaneously, an art which is only slowly mastered. At first Winston had laboriously memorized his speeches, which had drawn upon him Arthur Balfour's rebuke in debate that while Winston could deploy heavy artillery against his opponents, that artillery was "not very mobile." To counter this charge, Churchill tried speaking only with the help of notes carrying topical headings. This had not worked out in practice, leading to the embarrassing incident, and he went back to memorizing his speeches. This earned him an opponent's quip that he "spent the best years of his life preparing impromptu speeches." Only very slowly did speaking in the House come easily to Churchill. To the end of his life he lavished great care upon preparing for his major speeches there.

He worked hard at his job. In mastering the issues in the House he learned about poverty, not least from the benches opposite him. By early 1902 he had read Rowntree's study of poverty in York. He said candidly that he saw little glory in an Empire that allowed such human waste and misfortune at its center. He was not maturing into a typical Tory.

In his disregard for party conformity Winston was his father's son. In 1902 he had begun to work upon the research and writing of a biography of Lord Randolph, which he would complete in 1905. As he worked at this task, Winston grew convinced that his father had been badly used by the Tory Party. To filial piety was added ambition, for young Churchill was never inclined to wait in line behind men whose only claim to precedence was seniority; he was too able, energetic, imaginative and unconventional for that. A description of Winston set down at about this time survives:

> He is a little, square headed fellow of no very striking appearance, but of wit, intelligence, and originality. In mind and manner he is a strange replica of his father, with all his father's suddenness and assurance, and I should say more than his father's ability. . . . He has a power of writing Randolph never had . . . and he has education and political tradition. He interested me immensely.[1]

Churchill did not hesitate to challenge the most notable men in the House. Events would so fall out that his challenge would be most serious to the leadership of his own party.

High in the ranks of the Unionist Party, which had evolved in the years after Gladstone's advocacy of Irish Home Rule had lost a wing of the Liberals to association with the Tory Party, was one of the men who had led the Liberal Unionists over, Joseph Chamberlain. He attracted, and perhaps enjoyed, controversy. After making a fortune in business he had entered politics only in middle age. In his early political career Chamberlain had been a notable reforming, even radical, mayor of Birmingham. After his split with Gladstone, he seemed to move rapidly away from his early radicalism, earning Churchill's quip that he had been "first Fiery Red, then True Blue." Chamberlain was one of the most colorful politicians of his time, capable of delivering powerful, emotion-laden addresses. The appearance of this tall, handsome man was striking; he was always spotlessly attired, in white waistcoat, and with a fresh orchid always in his lapel. He also wore a monocle. This foppish exterior masked a decisive man capable of ruthless actions.

By 1902 Chamberlain was deeply concerned about the growing challenge to Britain's place in the world, by the emerging working-class challenge to the traditional parties, and by the seemingly lethargic response to these challenges by the Tory leader, Arthur Balfour. Chamberlain had become convinced that a system of protective tariffs with imperial preference would go far toward resolving international and domestic problems and at the same time would hold together the Empire by economic interest. To Chamberlain the issue was urgent. Britain needed such an economic tie to bind the self-governing colonies to her before it was too late. He believed that imperial pride and hoped-for economic benefits would capture wide public support. If Balfour would not lead the Unionist Party into this imperial promised land, Chamberlain was ready to lead whomever would follow him. Ever since the 1840s Britain had embraced the doctrine of free trade. It had served her well in the years she led the world in industrial development. Chamberlain believed those days were done. But free trade was an emotional issue and it had become part of the faith of Victorian England. To many, tariffs meant "Dear Bread" for the English laboring classes in a nation that imported much of its foodstuffs. Not surprisingly, Balfour doubted the political benefits of tariff reform, and this was a correct reading of public opinion. The Unionist Party contained its own dedicated free traders. None was stronger than Churchill, loyal to the policy of his father. With great dexterity, Balfour gained Chamberlain's resignation from the Cabinet in September, 1903, and dropped the most determined free traders at the same time by indicating support for a retaliatory tariff against foreign competitors. Balfour's dexterity was unrewarded for his middle way rallied few supporters; his party was splitting up behind him. Chamberlain stumped the country explaining that "Tariff Reform Means Work for All," a slogan that made little headway against the Liberal cry of "Dear Bread."

Among those Tories who pressed Balfour hardest for an unswerving commitment to free trade was Churchill. When Balfour declined it, Churchill refused to follow his leader. Winston even approached the Liberals about an electoral truce where Liberals and Unionist free traders would not oppose each other. Because party loyalty is highly prized and generally expected in modern Britain, Churchill's independence irritated those most dedicated to the Tory faith, the membership of his own constituency association. At the end of 1903 they informed him that he had forfeited their confidence and would not have their support in the next election. Essentially, he was now a man without a party. Churchill offered to resign his seat and fight a by-election, which the Oldham Unionists declined wisely, as an election would almost surely return a free trader.

This move bought Churchill time, but did not resolve his future. His father had broken with his party's leader and had forever lost his place in politics; the son would now have to take a step beyond the father. In April, 1904, Churchill indicated where he proposed to go. In a debate on a trade disputes bill, Winston delivered the most radical speech of his young political career; "of the reddest type," declared an enraged Tory newspaper. On May 31, 1904, Churchill, taking the final step, crossed the floor to join the Liberals. He sat down next to David Lloyd George. In 1905 Churchill published the biography of his father to favorable reviews. He was thirty years old and his debt to his father's memory was paid. Until now, Lord Randolph had led his son's career from the grave. But in May of 1904, Winston had passed beyond the guidance of that shade. In the next two decades of Churchill's life, he would be linked to the man beside whom he now sat. With David Lloyd George he was to journey far.

Tariff reform was only one of several shattering blows to Balfour's political fortunes. To reduce public drunkenness he had pushed a Licensing Act through Parliament; it led to many pub closings, but with compensation to owners who lost their licenses. To the strong British Temperance Movement and to most nonconformists generally this was paying the wages of sin. An Education Act of 1902, continuing state support for denominational schools, chiefly Church of England, roused more nonconformist discontent. A year earlier, the House of Lords had ruled in the Taff Vale Railway case that unions were liable without limit in suits brought against their members, in effect rendering strike action impossible without grave risk to union health and retirement funds. Thus almost every element of traditional Liberal and working-class sentiment was unhappy by 1905.

Balfour decided to resign and see if the Liberals, divided in attitude toward Empire, and with the skeleton of Home Rule rattling in their political closet, could unite to rule. They could. The promise of office had salved many political wounds and cemented many political unions before and would again. Sir Henry Campbell-Bannerman became Prime

Minister, and promptly made clear that Home Rule would not be an immediate issue. Thus many who left the Liberal fold in 1886 could return on the principle of free trade. Chamberlain had feared working-class politics; the Liberal chief whip, Herbert Gladstone, had embraced the new Labour Party, as it would shortly become, in an electoral arrangement that reduced three-cornered races and assured many Tory losses and some certain Labour victories. In the January 1906 elections the Tories, overwhelmed by a great vote for change, retained only 157 seats. The Liberals won 377 seats, along with 24 Lib-Labs, working-class candidates who ran under Liberal auspices. The new Labour Party had 29 members and the Irish Nationalist Party, nominal ally of a Liberal Party pledged to Irish Home Rule, had 83 seats.

Among the triumphant Liberals was Churchill, returned from a Manchester constituency. He accepted the position of under-secretary of the Colonial Office in Campbell-Bannerman's government. As the Colonial Secretary (Lord Elgin) sat in the upper house, Churchill would represent the department in the Commons. It was also a position where his experience in South Africa would be useful, for there were still consequences of the Boer War to be wrapped up. Indeed, in 1906 the Colonial Office was viewed as one of the more significant departments of state; fifty thousand dispatches and telegrams flowed into that office in a year from every corner of the world. The Prime Minister had given this great responsibility to a fellow Scotsman of long experience and careful judgment, whom Campbell-Bannerman trusted to avoid any such adventures as Chamberlain had entertained. Elgin had been Viceroy of India, and his father had directed Canada's evolution toward self-government; it was a popular appointment with everyone. Much different was the under-secretary. Churchill arrived at the Colonial Office with a reputation for being a young man in a hurry, as ambitious as he was able, decisive and quick to act, preferably before a large audience. Tories had not forgiven his change of party; the Prime Minister did not like him; in truth, few of the ruling class did. For their taste, Churchill was a little too obviously the self-made man.

The Liberal ministry could open its imperial record from strength. They could negotiate a final settlement with the Boers with most of the strong cards in the deck already secured for them by their Tory predecessors. The Unionist peace with the Boers contained a clause leaving open the native-franchise question until after self-government was working in the Transvaal and Orange Free State. This conveniently put the troublesome issue of the Black vote beyond recall; the Liberals could rejoice to find their hands tied. But the Liberal commitment to colonial responsible government was strong in conviction and party tradition alike. Liberal attitudes toward the Empire were also informed by a strong sense that it should be a great moral force on the side of progress. Churchill would himself write of looking forward to larger brotherhoods and more exact standards of social justice. But in fact it was the "looking forward" that always gave Englishmen trouble. Colonial peoples anticipated more exact standards of social justice with the next sunrise; the horizon as seen from London was always a more distant one for the 400 million people it governed in an area covering one-fifth of the world's territory.

The Tories, following Lord Milner's good advice from South Africa, had already provided that in due time the two Boer republics would become self-governing. The Liberals decided to act boldly for Anglo-Boer reconciliation and accelerate this process. Elections in the Transvaal produced majorities for the Boer parties of Louis Botha and his associates who had led the Boers in the field against Britain only a few years earlier. A new act in 1909 set the groundwork for the Union of South Africa, regulating provincial and Union governmental relations. Reconciliation appeared successful. But the Union was non-federal, and Sir Charles Dilke warned that the anomalous status of Blacks, voting in Cape Colony, but not in the Dutch republics, could hardly strengthen "the Imperial fabric in an Empire where there are 360 millions of colored people...." Yet to override the Boer color-bar would be to override the principle of colonial self-government, and Australia, at least, would be sure to protest, and possibly New Zealand and Canada as well. Yet few Englishmen were ready to ask if this sort of an Empire was worth its price.

Another South African problem was the importation of Chinese to work in the mines, under conditions that were compared to slavery. The government acted to stop such importation and to improve the condition of the Chinese already in South Africa. Investigation of the whole problem revealed that Lord Milner, whose tenure as High Commissioner had ended in 1905, had allowed illegal floggings. During a debate in the Commons in 1906 to censure Milner, young Churchill had enraged the Tories yet further by combining condemnation of Milner with what the fallen proconsul's admirers viewed as a patronizing, even insulting, plea for leniency. It was, in truth, a graceless speech, but Churchill was becoming a convenient object of Tory attack because he tactlessly criticized Tory shortcomings that the gentlemen of England preferred to pass over in silence.

In 1907 when a colonial conference was convened, much of the responsibility for its functioning fell to Churchill. Liberal opposition to the dreams of Tory Imperialists, who sought centralization and integration, joined with growing nationalism in the self-governing colonies to assure that the 1907 conference should endorse, even if only tacitly, the values of autonomy and disintegration. It was quickly agreed that the next such conference would be called imperial and not colonial, and the Prime Minister, not the Colonial Secretary, should preside. These were sign posts toward political equality between mother country and self-governing dominions. Relations were not entirely smooth; ambitious ministers from the colonies did not get imperial preference from the mother country; hopeful British ministers did not get much in the way of imperial defense from the self-governing dominions. For by 1907, the balance of world power politics was increasingly in British minds when they surveyed their imperial obligations, Britain's interests, and the restless state of great-power relations. The year 1907 also saw Britain and Russia settle outstanding issues in Asia, both great powers negotiating the settlement with one eye cocked toward central Europe.

Churchill, tired by the conference, decided upon an African trip where he could mix business with pleasure. Before he left, he significantly attended French army maneuvers in the summer of 1907, having seen the German army the year before. He was accompanied to France by F. E. Smith, a rising Tory politician who would remain a close friend until Smith's death in 1930. Smith's brilliant legal mind, razor-sharp tongue, and ruthless disregard of the conventional appealed to Churchill even as they repelled and antagonized others. The two men were truly close, each standing as godfather to the other's only son. The two men shared a readiness to assault life with an energy that few could equal.

Hardly was Churchill off to Africa than his appalled personal secretary was reporting fourteen-hour days spent preparing memoranda under a broiling Red Sea sun for dispatch to a Colonial Secretary who was by 1907 probably happy to have Churchill out of sight, if still impossible to put out of mind. The problem between the two men was

Winston's unabashed desire to enter the Cabinet, perhaps across the body of his ostensible chief. Churchill's administrative unconventionality also upset Elgin, although the older man never denied the younger's great administrative abilities. By the time Churchill returned from Africa he had outgrown his place in the government. His lack of patience in seeking tasks more equal to his ability cost him popularity. The speed with which his restless mind took up a given issue, exhausted it—often with much oratorical accompaniment—and passed on to quite a different topic earned Winston a reputation for instability and even drew accusations of exploiting issues solely for political gain. Brilliant and imaginative Churchill was; but his critics charged he lacked the staying-power for high political office.

Quite a different view of Churchill's abilities was held by Herbert Henry Asquith, who succeeded the dying Campbell-Bannerman as Prime Minister in April, 1908. A general reshuffling of the government followed. Lloyd George succeeded Asquith as Chancellor of the Exchequer, which left open the Presidency of the Board of Trade. Churchill accepted this position at once, but also with some regret. His experience to date was imperial—army and Colonial Office—rather than domestic. He had rejected considering the Local Government Board with the comment that he refused to be shut up in a soup kitchen with Mrs. Sidney Webb. But he would have to discover the significance of social issues, and the Board of Trade responsibilities provided the opportunity. He joined one of the most gifted of British Cabinets, including Richard B. Haldane, the reforming War Secretary, John Morley at the India Office, Reginald McKenna at the Admiralty, and Sir Edward Grey as Foreign Secretary,

Prior to the First World War (and for a time after) a member of Parliament, when he accepted an office of profit under the Crown, had to vacate his seat and stand for re-election. This tradition from an earlier era of constitutional thinking, which stressed the independence of the legislature from the executive, was to give Churchill trouble. Narrowly defeated when he stood for re-election in his Manchester constituency, he accepted the offer of a safe seat in Dundee, a citadel of Scottish Liberalism, and a constituency with a large working-class electorate. He was duly returned as member on May 9, 1908. He hoped it would prove a life constituency, but this was not to be.

If Churchill was to be ultimately disappointed in his new constituency, he was to be abundantly fortunate in marriage the same year. On September 12, he wed Clementine Hozier at St. Margaret's Westminister, the parish church of the House of Commons. A beautiful and gifted woman, his wife became a strong and loyal helpmate in a marriage which ended only upon Winston's death. Their mutual love, constant and abiding, did not flag with time. Winston set down his own testimony when he wrote, "I married and lived happily ever afterwards."

Perhaps a story from the darkest days of World War II best illustrates the character of "Clemmie" Churchill. In June 1940, after the desperate evacuation of the British army from Dunkirk, the full force of Hitler's arms were turned upon the collapsing French forces. Churchill wished to fly to France to try to impart some of his courage to the French government, and to assure them of a continuing British effort in the war. Churchill's advisers thought the flight to France through skies now dominated by the German Air Force much too dangerous for the British Prime Minister; even the weather conditions were hostile to a safe flight. When Winston refused to be deflected by their fears, his advisers asked Clemmie to intervene. Her response was short: "There is a battle on; other men are flying: he must go." And he did.

The Presidency of the Board of Trade brought Churchill for the first time directly into contact with one of the main tasks of the Liberal government and with one of the central themes of British history in the twentieth century: the movement of social reform toward the eventual achievement of the Welfare State. This was unnatural ground to Winston, whose life had been spent in that side of Britain that looked outward upon world Empire and the power politics of international affairs. Yet domestic reform and social thinking had been in a period of notable evolution since the time of Winston's birth, and the bold and novel always had appeal to him.

Churchill pitched into social reform with vigor. He was a formidable gain to the forces of social progress for he possessed the significant assets of working hard, and being able to put programs through Cabinet and Commons alike articulately and efficiently. He was lucky in his Permanent Secretary, the chief civil servant, in the Board of Trade. This was Hubert Llewellyn-Smith, a man of great ability. In Churchill's two years as President, the Board of Trade carried through legislation to improve conditions in sweated trades, to create labor exchanges, and contributed to the great landmark bill on national insurance which would become law in 1911.

The sweated-trade legislation was designed to set legal minimum rates for workers on piece-work in virtually unorganized industries where the worst cases of labor exploitation, particularly of women, occurred. The Labor Exchanges facilitated finding employment. This long overdue step of rationalization was instantly successful. It also illustrates Churchill's approach to social issues of the day, and his desire for an efficient, well-functioning and decent British society. His greatness as a social reformer lay in his energy and his accomplishment rather than in his vision of a new sort of society.

David Lloyd George once in a graphic scene described the arrival at his ministry of employers' and employees' delegations. His description left no doubt which side he was on: the work-scarred laborers with the strains of hard years etched into the lines of their faces, not the well-to-do employers. His Welsh nonconformist youth amid rural poverty made Lloyd George an instinctive man of the people, even though he was not intimately acquainted with industrial, urban social problems. Churchill was never this sort of man; his radicalism sprang from his imagination and his unwillingness to be trammeled by conformity to tradition. Churchill was a humane and compassionate man; perhaps in the end he preserved these qualities better than Lloyd George. But Churchill did not plan social revolution, only reformation of the society he knew and that had provided him with opportunity. Many men who dreamed mightier dreams of social reformation than Winston did far less than he to better the lot of their fellow men.

The National Insurance Act was the social landmark of Asquith's government. Of the members of that government, its enactment owes most to Lloyd George, and then to Churchill. The unemployment insurance part was chiefly Winston's concern. By 1914 it covered about 2,250,000 workers in the building and engineering trades, notably vulnerable to fluctuations in the national economy. Lloyd George's part set up health insurance for most people who worked, with contributions from worker, employer, and the State supporting the payments to the sick. Both parts of the bill had set rates of contribution on a scale, and set rates of payment under described categories. Some of the Labour Party objected to the set rates of contribution and wished the whole cost paid from general taxation, but trade unionists were inclined to accept the charges because they strengthened the workman's claim to receive benefit as his right. This probably was a good reading of public sentiment at the time.

Social reform, along with imperial defense, was to lead into political reform, indeed into constitutional crisis. The great victory of the forces of progress in 1906 had touched the House of Lords not at all. That mainly hereditary house contained a Conservative majority as great as the government majority in the Commons. The Lords had accepted the Trade Disputes Act of 1906, which reversed the Taff Vale decision by granting unions immunity from liability for members' actions; this remedied a working-class grievance the upper house dare not stand out against. But Liberal bills designed to meet other election pledges got rough handling; education, voting, licensing, and land reform bills all died under the lordly ax. Such blatantly partisan activity was defended on the grounds that the House of Lords was acting as watchdog of the Constitution, rejecting unsuitable legislation. The problem was that only Liberal, and never Tory legislation seemed unsuitable to their lordships. Indeed, the Unionist peers seem to have become quite carried away by the exercise of political power, albeit negative, an exercise that had been in steady decline from the seventeenth century.

Lloyd George in particular was unhappy. He needed large new sums for his 1909 budget to meet sharply higher costs for social welfare programs and naval shipbuilding. In his budget he sought new revenues from higher death duties, distinguishing for purposes of taxation between earned and unearned income, especially unearned increments in land value, and he added a new supertax on very high incomes. He also increased tobacco and liquor taxes. While the actual rates of taxation were mild by later standards, it was a budget that to the enraged wealthy, especially the landed wealthy, was a direct attack upon them—and nobody so represented the landed wealthy as did the House of Lords. By ancient constitutional custom the Commons controlled finance; for the Lords to reject the budget would thus precipitate a political and constitutional crisis. This is exactly what the Lords did; perhaps it is what Lloyd George wished them to do.

The government now appealed to the people against the Lords in a general election in January, 1910. The result brought joy only to the Irish. The government obtained its majority, but one vastly reduced from 1906. In a Commons with 275 Liberals and 273 Unionists, the balance lay with 40 Labour and 82 Irish members. Clearly, Irish support would all but commit the government to honor the Liberal Party's ancient pledge of Home Rule. Now the budget went through. But at this point in the spring of 1910, Edward VII died. His son, George V, found himself King in the midst of a constitutional crisis. For the government insisted upon a Parliament Act that would curb the Lords' power, specifically ending any role by the upper house in money bills, and setting a two-year limit on the Lords' veto of other legislation in exchange for shortening the statutory maximum life of Parliaments from seven to five years. The only way to thrust this unpalatable medicine down the Lords' throats was by threatening that the King would create as many new peers as needed to carry the bill if the present membership of the house refused to. George V renewed his father's understanding with Asquith: the royal pledge of creations would only follow another election. So in December, 1910 the voters ratified their earlier decision, returning 272 Liberals, 272 Unionists, 84 Irish, and 42 Labour. In August of 1911, faced with a humiliating inflation in their number, the Lords themselves accepted the bill, 131 to 114, overcoming a revolt of their own least-enlightened members. Much of the conduct in the Lords' affair and the passage of the Parliament Act of 1911, which only ratified the fact that Britain was by now a democratic state, would appear to be ludicrous were it not so serious. For it revealed a significant segment of the ruling class ready to repeal the twentieth century and it disclosed an appalling lack of leadership, much less statesmanship, in the upper ranks of the Tory Party.

If short on reason, the Tories were long on emotion, and raged at the most obvious targets, Lloyd George and Churchill. To angry Tories, Churchill, the descendant of dukes, was now the foulest sort of traitor to his class. Yet Churchill's conduct in the crisis was not without its ambiguity. Unyielding in his public speeches, he advised Asquith to persevere, yet he also approached the Tories to explore the possibility of an electoral truce or even coalition. Lloyd George went even further, but with equal lack of success. Party politics sank to a new low of bitterness.

In 1910 Churchill became Home Secretary, a significant Cabinet promotion in recognition of the great weight he carried in the government. He replaced Herbert Gladstone, whom Churchill thought lacked vigor in enforcing wage minimums in sweated trades. The Home Office required vigor, for its functions were numerous: law and order, police and prisons, justice, advice to the Crown on mercy, juvenile wards of the state and the public safety, including preserving order in strike situations.

This last scarred Churchill's reputation; strikes were numerous in the period, and violence not unknown. When a miners' strike at Tonypandy in the Rhonddha Valley in 1910 threatened to get beyond local authorities' capacity to assure order, they asked Churchill for troops. Wisely he sent first police reinforcements, but also troops. He kept close control on their use. Although order was restored without serious incident, yet there lives on in Labour Party folklore an image of Churchill the murderer of miners at Tonypandy. This longlived myth probably came about because of the transference to Tonypandy of Churchill's conduct in the railway strike of 1911. Here Churchill seized the initiative in mobilizing and issuing ammunition to 50,000 troops, who were distributed at strategic points throughout the country. He also authorized the military commanders to act if necessary without first receiving requests for aid from local civil authorities. These were unwise actions, to say the least. There was one nasty incident when soldiers shot two men, admittedly in provocative circumstances. The rising Labour leader Ramsay MacDonald's criticism of Churchill was not unjust, namely that had Churchill a bit more knowledge of how to handle masses of men under stressful strike conditions, some of the difficulties accompanying the railway strike might have been avoided. Indeed, Churchill was not alone in this; in the whole Cabinet only the little-regarded lightweight, John Burns, knew anything about a strike at first hand, and only Lloyd George showed much skill at getting around confrontation and to the conference table.

Lloyd George blamed Winston's behavior upon his instinct to dramatize events, and then to believe in his own dramatic presentation—a fair criticism. Thus tenure at the Home Office did not diminish Churchill's public reputation for erratic behavior. In a difficult London dock strike in 1911 he played a notably moderating and helpful role, but soon he was all too obviously present at a police shoot-out with a pair of anarchists. This trivial affair hardly required the Home Secretary in the street directing operations, with the Horse Artillery summoned up in reserve. Churchill never lost this element of child-like romantic dramatization in his character even into old age. But what became part of the lovable eccentricity in an elder statesman could appear as a reckless taste for sabre and gunsmoke in an ex-cavalry officer become driving minister in high and responsible office while still well short of his fortieth birthday. Neither Labour nor Tory politicians now trusted him.

Yet, as so often with Winston, underneath these surface storms lay a strong, sound administrative record quite lost from public view. Imprisonment was one experience Churchill did know at first hand, and he had shown his feelings by promptly escaping. His prison reforms as Home Secretary were sound and significant. Notably, he initiated legal changes to substitute fines for incarceration upon minor infractions, particularly concerning drunkenness—a significant social problem in Britain before World War I—and allowing time to pay fines before jailing. This kept a lot of men out of jail. Churchill improved conditions and opportunities for training for those who were in jail. He also carried through legislation concerning offenders aged sixteen to twenty-one, restricting types of penalties, and noting fairly that such penalties normally fell only on working-class boys who were punished for behavior that Oxford and Cambridge undergraduates indulged in free of legal penalty. Churchill was, in fact, a progressive, reforming Home Secretary.

The passage of the Parliament Act of 1911 opened the door for accomplishment of that Irish Home Rule to which Gladstone had pledged the Liberal Party in 1886. This Irish issue had worked havoc upon the forces of progress in Britain down until 1906. Even more misfortune was now due. The fatal bar to an Irish settlement was the northern province of Ulster. There, the population was Protestant and industrialized, in contrast to the predominantly rural Catholic southern Ireland. Protestant Ulster had watched with growing fear the long erosion of the traditional Protestant ascendancy in Ireland, and was determined not to accept a Catholic ascendancy. The depth of this emotion was underrated by the leader of the Irish Nationalist Party, John Redmond, who deeply believed in conciliation and the parliamentary process. Just as he believed the English would grant Ireland Home Rule, so he believed Ulster could be conciliated. If Redmond's shortcomings were his very moderation and failure to grasp the depth of emotion in Ulster, the Tory leadership's failing was its lack of moderation. Unwisely, the Tories thought that opposition to Home Rule could be exploited for political gain. This was a card Lord

Randolph Churchill had not hesitated to play in 1886. But by 1910 the Tories were committing themselves to the support of men in Ulster who were prepared to go beyond constitutional means—if necessary to resort to arms. If men could be found in Ulster ready to resist Home Rule, men could be found in southern Ireland who would bear arms to achieve it, and perhaps not stop there. Ireland was splitting into two armed camps behind the back of the pacific Mr. Redmond.

After the passage of the Parliament Act of 1911, the Ulster Unionists stated that they would ignore any Home Rule Bill passed into law and would set up their own Ulster government. Sir Edward Carson, the Irish Unionist leader, described Home Rule as a conspiracy directed against a free people. Neither Asquith nor Redmond seemed to recognize how serious these words were. Balfour's forced retirement in 1911 as Tory leader and replacement by Andrew Bonar Law did not help the forces of reason. The new Tory leader announced that he could not imagine any length of resistance to which Ulster would go that he could not support. Either Bonar Law's imagination was remarkably limited or he was prepared to support insurrection. In any case the statement encouraged recklessness rather than reasonableness.

Asquith faithfully carried his Home Rule Bill through the House of Commons in 1912 to expected defeat in the Lords; this left the Lords' veto to run until 1914 while Ulster raised and armed a volunteer force against that day. Neither Asquith nor Redmond wanted to resort to coercion and launch Home Rule upon bayonets, but the alternative of appearing to do nothing about the Ulster Volunteers undermined the government's authority. Early in 1914 Asquith and Redmond offered Ulster an option to vote itself out of Home Rule for six years, which the Unionists spurned.

While the government was undoing itself with moderation, Unionist and Anglo-Irish army officers stationed in Ireland concluded they would be faced with imposing Home Rule by force, and preferred to resign their commissions. This episode, misnamed the Curragh Mutiny, was at root the consequence of hysterical prejudice in the officers and blundering incompetence in their superiors who put a foolish set of alternatives to them. It was patched up, but added its damage to the government's reputation. George V himself intervened at Asquith's request to bring the various groups into conference at the eleventh hour in July, 1914. The conference failed; Home Rule would become law within a few weeks. But when it became law, it was with the provision that it would not come into operation until the end of World War I, for that conflict had intervened at the last minute and all parliamentary parties agreed to set aside the Irish question until its conclusion; most expected a short war.

Churchill's role in the Ulster crisis did him further public harm. In private he was concerned to meet Ulster's apprehensions if at all possible, but conceded that Ulster's rights could not be allowed to override the rest of Ireland's interest. But in public Churchill was provoked beyond such judicious weighing of rights and wrongs. He was enraged by the Ulster Volunteers' readiness to defy the constitution by force. He deplored Asquith's irresolution, which Winston believed could only serve to encourage defiance of the government's right to govern, a right sustained by three successive elections within five years. Churchill would negotiate if he could, but not at gun-point. Thus Winston, since 1911 head of the Admiralty, had ordered warships to Irish ports in the spring of 1914 and, in a speech at Bradford, declared that, if the issue was to be parliamentary government or civil violence, he for one was ready to put the matter to the test. Those Tories who had been most reckless in voicing support of the Ulster Volunteers were the most loud in accusing Winston of plotting a bloodbath, a pogrom, in Ulster. Churchill's sharp reply that such accusations constituted a vote of censure by the criminal classes upon the police was all the more provocative for its accuracy. Asquith, roused at last to action, now intervened to recall the warships and lower the political temperature. But the Tories, particularly Bonar Law, believed as firmly that Churchill had plotted a massacre as Labourites believed he had murdered miners at Tonypandy. Churchill had rather more moral courage than Asquith; he rightly insisted that no constitutional government can allow itself to be coerced by threats of insurrection. The behavior of the Tory leadership, narrow, mindless and reckless, did not entitle them to cast stones at Churchill. But they did, and in all truth Churchill made himself into an attractive target by his lack of tactical skill, his public flamboyance, and his dramatic gestures. This cost him much, for he badly needed widespread public confidence if he was to lead successfully one of the service departments in a time of national crisis.

Notes to Chapter II

1 W. S. Blunt, *Diaries,* quoted in R. S. Churchill, *Winston S. Churchill* (Houghton Mifflin, Boston, 1967), II, 68.

CHAPTER THREE

The Young Warrior: 1911—1915

By the beginning of the twentieth century, splendid isolation was for Britain going the way of the splendor that had been Rome's. Once it was quipped that George III had granted Edward Gibbon a pension so that the great historian would not write a British sequel to his *Decline and Fall of the Roman Empire.* Imperialists were no longer amused. The Boer War had revealed a distressing amount of hostility toward Britain, and the British Empire was beginning to look like a giant hostage to fortune rather than a great reservoir of strength. The rising power that had been most obnoxious in its delight in Boer victories had been Germany. This upset British imperialists for many reasons. The racism that underlay so much of imperialism argued that it was the destiny of the "Teutonic" peoples—notably the British, Germans, and Americans—jointly to bear the burden of holding dominion over the rest of the world's population. To anyone familiar with the composition of the American population—to cite only the most obvious case—the concept appears on its face ridiculous. Yet so real did it seem then that the famous Rhodes Scholarships were founded upon this concept.

Not surprisingly, then, the first effort of British imperialists was to come to terms with Germany. At the turn of century, Joseph Chamberlain attempted such a settlement. He failed. The acquisition of great power through industrialization, imperial expansion, and in some cases national unification and territorial aggrandizement had worked upon the essentially narrow, traditional minds of the old European ruling classes to produce an unquestioning arrogance that would ultimately destroy the old Europe. And nowhere in Europe was this arrogance more evident and less intelligent than in the new imperial Germany that had risen upon three centuries of Prussian blood and iron. The German leaders believed that Britain was the suppliant and must meet their terms, sooner or later. They were in no hurry to settle outstanding grievances.

Of these grievances, two particularly distressed Englishmen: the new German navy and German economic imperialism in the Turkish Empire. The backbone of Germany had always been its army; a great navy was something new, the creation of a power seeking its place in the sun. The German Kaiser, William II, Queen Victoria's grandson, had proclaimed that Germany's destiny now lay upon the high seas. Admiral von Tirpitz, a man of great energy and political skill, had steered a series of naval laws through the imperial legislature by popularizing the navy among the rising German industrialists and the middle class. Horrified Englishmen saw the first real challenge to Britain's naval supremacy since the days of Napoleon. The vehicle of German economic expansion was the Berlin-to-Baghdad Railway, a grandiose scheme seriously extended in 1899. This would come uncomfortably close to the Persian Gulf and the Indian Ocean beyond, both traditionally British lakes.

The Balfour government had decided that any friend was better than no friend. If Germany's leaders were unsociable, the French had been showing quite a different attitude, first indicated in the peaceful conclusion of the Fashoda incident on Britain's terms. Balfour's Foreign Secretary, Lord Lansdowne, concluded negotiations with the willing French in 1904 and achieved a cordial understanding, the "Entente Cordiale." In detail, each nation accorded the other a free hand in an area of interest, Britain in Egypt, and France in Morocco, and settled a few lesser colonial issues. On paper this hardly constituted an alliance, yet each nation was enlisting the other's support in case of difficulties with Germany. By 1904, each nation had its hopes, and its fears, on that subject.

Already Britain had taken out an imperial insurance policy in the Far East, signing a treaty with Japan in 1902. Thus the new entente was strained by the Russo-Japanese War of 1904-05, which saw Britain's ally Japan victorious over France's ally, Russia. Yet the long-term loser was Germany, and its allies, Austria and Italy. Frustrated in Asia, shaken by a revolution in 1905, Tsarist Russia turned increasingly back toward Europe, very much as France wished. Britain could now resolve past differences with a Russia no longer pressing upon British-ruled Asia. An Anglo-Russian agreement in 1907 in fact completed the choosing up of sides in Europe until Italy's defection from the Triple Alliance in 1914 and 1915. Yet few people, least of all Englishmen, saw anything so definite in 1907. The Liberal Foreign Minister, Sir Edward Grey, had indeed continued and extended Lansdowne's policy. When Germany had challenged France's role in Morocco, the Liberal government had stood with France at the Algeciras Conference in 1906. Grey allowed Anglo-French military conversations, while telling France that he could make no political commitment to aid her in a war with Germany. One might perhaps call such an arrangement a binding non-commitment.

Only slowly did the Asquith government come to recognize all that such a step entailed. After the Algeciras Conference a quiet descended upon international relations outside the confines of Slavonic Europe, where a hundred local feuds fed the fires of Austrian and Russian hostility toward each other's ambitions in that unhappy region. Not until 1911 was Britain directly affected by her commitments, and the site of trouble was again Morocco. A native revolt had led to armed French intervention to protect her interests, when, in July, 1911, the German warship *Panther* had arrived in the Moroccan port of Agadir. This was followed by a crude demand that Germany be compensated with the entire French Congo in return for acknowledging France's free hand in Morocco. Such pool-hall tactics were unwelcome at the imperial baccarat table. Further, the initial British impression was that the *Panther* announced a German desire for a naval base at Agadir, uncomfortably close to Gibraltar. An angry Lloyd George, who saw his social programs threatened by the costs of naval competition with Germany, had gone to the Mansion House, London's City Hall, and in a speech all but threatened war. A settlement was patched up and Germany paid off with a narrow strip of Congo territory, but the ramifications of the *Panther's* leap reached deep into the British government.

Until the Agadir crisis, both Lloyd George and Churchill, the two most energetic members of the Cabinet, had together labored in the fields of social reform. Both had opposed the vastly increased expenditures demanded by the naval competition with Germany. Now both seem to have come over to the position that there did indeed exist a German naval menace to Britain.

The forces within England that held this attitude by 1911 were strong and influential. The imperialists had long been concerned, but the British Army, not the Royal Navy, was the service most associated with the imperialists. The army, strongly influenced by the rationalizing views of the imperialists, was ready to embrace strategic planning and co-operation with France. Within the Royal Navy the emphasis was quite different. The dominating figure in the senior service had been Admiral Sir John Fisher, First Sea Lord from 1904 to 1910. This man of demonic energy, who lived, indeed thrived, amid intrigue and controversy, had led the Royal Navy into a revolution in matériel. In 1906, he had launched his triumph, *H.M.S. Dreadnought,* the first all-big-gun warship. Because older ironclad warships carried guns of small caliber along their sides, much like the old sailing men of war, and mounted only a few guns of the largest caliber on their main decks, they were at a great disadvantage against the *Dreadnought,* which in combat could overpower older ships outside the range of their smaller guns. The only adequate response to the *Dreadnought* was to build ships like her, and an intense naval building race ensued, led by Britain and Germany. Fisher's solution to the German naval threat was to build as many such ships as possible, concentrating them in the North Sea for the moment of Armageddon. Planning, Fisher believed, was something that went on in an admiral's head, and went on best when unfettered by contact with generals of any nation and certainly not with foreign admirals.

Although Balfour had created, and Asquith continued, a Committee of Imperial Defense—the name makes clear its concern—presided over by the Prime Minister, ostensibly for the purpose of joint planning among politicians, generals and admirals, in fact by 1911 not much had been achieved. Indeed, the generals had little concern in joint planning with the navy, even though the army had received a thorough-going reformation, including a functional general staff to provide it with a brain, under the guidance of the brilliant War Secretary, R. B. Haldane. The *Panther* episode had led to a flurry of activity, which revealed that British and French armies seemed to have a well developed plan in case of a conflict with Germany, but that the Royal Navy's plans were still fermenting in the mind of Fisher's able but unfortunately inarticulate successor, Sir Arthur Wilson.

This revelation led Asquith to make two decisions: to inform the navy that it would have to support the Anglo-French military strategy—that is, transport a British Expeditionary Force to France— and to send a new broom to sweep the Admiralty into war planning. Haldane wanted the job, but Asquith did not wish thus to insult the admirals. Yet the Prime Minister needed a new First Lord who could not be frightened by the admirals, abashed by the technical problems of naval affairs, or too weak to push through sweeping reforms. Churchill obviously met these qualifications and he wanted the job. He got it.

In October of 1911, Churchill gave up domestic reform for dread-noughts and admirals, which he considered a happy change. His critics, however, alleged that he got out of home affairs because he could not beat Lloyd George in his native field. To his new task he brought a mandate for a change and certain preconceptions. Although he was trained as a soldier, he had long regarded the navy as Britain's chief military instrument, essentially a defensive instrument. But Churchill was never a warmonger, and he had much of his father's isolationism. Important for the future was Churchill's view of his office. The Order-in-Council that described the duties of the First Lord of the Admiralty made him responsible to the Crown and to Parliament for all the business of the Admiralty. Churchill accepted this in its fullest sense, and was prepared to exercise a broad authority. Asquith, who wanted reform in the service department, did not discourage Winston.

From the first, Churchill set out to know every aspect of the Admiralty's work. In his first year and a half as First Lord he was 182 days at sea. Nearly every important naval station and warship within reach was examined at first hand. But 182 days at sea do not make a sailor or a First Lord, and Churchill was wise enough to seek expert advice. He chose to consult the retired Admiral Fisher, with whom he carried on a flamboyant correspondence. But Winston quickly dumped Sir Arthur Wilson when the First Sea Lord would not accept the idea of a naval staff, which he believed suited only to armies and not to naval affairs. Sir Francis Bridgeman, a colorless man, followed Wilson. The new appointment did not work either, because Bridgeman and Churchill could not agree where one job left off and the other took up. Consequently, in late 1912, Prince Louis of Battenberg became Churchill's third professional associate. Such rapid change had attracted criticism, especially that Churchill was going too far into professional matters. But Winston believed his mandate required this action; besides, he could not be restrained anyway, as his energy and interest alike were too great. Many professional officers, navy and army, in two world wars, could never reconcile themselves to the role in the professional side of the services which Churchill took to himself. It was indeed rather unique in the annals of modern parliamentary government, but the heart of the matter was that Churchill was an unique man.

A man who breaks the normal conventions will certainly attract criticism and must make the record of his accomplishment his defense. Churchill accomplished much as First Lord. His first change was for a staff system. Early in 1912 an Admiralty War Staff was at last organized, with a chief who was responsible to the First Sea Lord. The staff's duty was to provide for the special study of the operational side of naval affairs. While this step was much admired at the time, there were serious deficiencies. The staff was strictly an advisory body, and suffered from the Royal Navy's acute shortage of trained staff officers. A Staff College was started in 1912 to supply this latter deficiency, but it took time. In truth, the Fisher era had bequeathed to Churchill a navy that had undergone a technical revolution but not a personnel revolution. The upper ranks of the Royal Navy were seriously short of first-class talent, and some of what talent was available, like Herbert Richmond who became Assistant Director of Naval Operations, was restricted by limitations of personality from full use. Churchill's best find was David Beatty, whom he rescued from half-pay, made his naval secretary, and pushed on to his notable career as a fighting admiral and, ultimately, a distinguished First Sea Lord. But in general, Winston towered over his professional advisers in sheer energy and breadth of mind, which partly accounts for the vast role in naval affairs that he came to play.

The naval service over which Churchill had come to preside had a long and glorious tradition that imparted confidence to British naval officers, but also complacency and a reluctance to face needed changes. A modern admiral has written that "naval officers were serious, professionally competent in seamanship and the operation of their weapons, but unimaginative, conformist and uncritical."[1] Churchill, unwilling to allow this to dismay him, vigorously pushed reform at every level of the navy. As First Lord, Winston had also to consider the opinions of King George V, who had spent many years in the naval service and always followed naval affairs with an informed interest. At least twice Winston and his monarch disagreed upon the subject of suitable names for battleships. Churchill proposed on one occasion the name *Cromwell*, but the King firmly vetoed the name of the great regicide. It was not in truth a very tactful suggestion to make, even to a constitutional monarch. On another occasion Churchill proposed the name *Pitt*. The King replied that this raised "the danger of the men giving the ship nicknames of ill-conditioned words rhyming with it." A shocked Winston, who could be very naive at times, responded "I think that unworthy of the royal mind."[2] But the King's observation, based on long naval experience, was surely sound on this point, and Churchill abandoned the proposed name.

Fresh from battling for domestic social reform, and urged on by Fisher, Winston enthusiastically attacked Lower Deck problems. An advocate of careers open to talent, Churchill reformed punishments, improved legal procedures, widened opportunity for leave, raised pay, and greatly broadened promotion opportunities. Churchill could claim to have done as much to modernize personnel practices in the Royal Navy as any other man.

In shipbuilding, Churchill carried the development of the dreadnought-type warship to its fullest extent prior to the outbreak of World War I by providing for the *Queen Elizabeth* class of five battleships. These mounted a 15-inch naval rifle, greater than any gun previously used, which in turn meant a yet larger battleship to carry the huge weapons. Fisher urged Churchill to go whole hog—Fisher's picturesque expression was *"totus porcus"*—and give these ships unrivaled speed, too. Churchill needed little urging, but the decision was of vast importance, for it involved abandoning coal for oil fuel. Much argued for such a decision: greater thermal efficiency, which could be translated into higher speed more quickly achieved, vastly greater ease of bulk-handling, greater sea-range for equivalent weight, significant saving in manpower and back-breaking labor. One great argument opposed: Britain was sufficient in coal and utterly deficient in oil supplies; to convert to oil meant basing Britain's naval power upon foreign sources.

With the U.S. Navy already building oil-fired battleships there was really little choice; Winston plumped for oil. Next, to get that oil, a Royal Commission was proposed by Churchill and Fisher was drafted to head it. Acting upon its report, and in order to secure a safe, adequate, cheap supply, the government in 1914 bought the controlling share of what became the Anglo-Iranian Oil Company. Thus began for Britain, which had risen to industrial preeminence upon coal in the nineteenth century, a revolution in fuel energy sources that has not yet run its course.

The imaginative Churchill was always fascinated by technical innovation; few innovations so raised his enthusiasm as the airplane. He was probably the first prominent English politician to fly, surely the first to handle an airplane's controls, before his wife accomplished the notable feat of grounding Winston. Given his cavalryman's approach to things, Clemmie's judgment seems wise and her exercise of will must have been monumental. Churchill correctly rated the airplane a better bet than the airship, despite the Second Sea Lord, Admiral Jellicoe's enthusiasm for the latter. More quickly than his admirals Churchill also saw that planes could more than scout—they could bomb. In 1913 *H.M.S. Hermes* was commissioned as Britain's first aircraft carrier, and when war came in 1914 the Royal Navy had nearly a hundred aircraft, including seaplanes, and was well ahead of the army in air development.

Churchill's contribution to preparing the Royal Navy to meet the challenge of war was clearly great, but his accomplishment cannot obscure his failures. For example, when war came Britain did not have a first-class naval base facing the North Sea that was truly secure, especially from submarine penetration. The best potential base, and eventually the chief base in the two World Wars, was Scapa Flow in the Orkneys, north of Scotland. Although Churchill recognized its potential significance, he did not secure its development. But far more serious even than this was Churchill's failure to achieve the purpose for which he had become First Lord: when war came, the Royal Navy did not have an effective, sound operational planning organization that fed directly into the highest decision-making level. The cause of this failure lay in no small measure upon professional traditionalism in an officer corps inclined to believe that the Nelson touch, the inspired fighting admiral, would still do the job in an era of constant technological revolution. It would not; the Nelson touch had died as a method of directing the higher conduct of naval war with the age of sail. The Royal Navy in 1914 thus had the worst of both worlds: neither a Nelson nor an effective modern substitute. In truth, Churchill tried hard enough to be the Nelson, and by sheer energy and vision nearly succeeded. But in the end he sustained overwhelming personal catastrophe, in no small measure because the instrument of war he had forged was defective. He cannot escape his share of the responsibility, for which he paid the full penalty.

Churchill had become distinctly unpopular in Germany. Early in 1912 the British government dispatched Haldane to Germany to investigate the possibility of securing a reduction in the naval shipbuilding race. It inflamed sentiment in both countries and cost a great deal of money, which the Liberal Cabinet would cheerfully have saved or spent on social welfare programs. The day before Haldane arrived in Berlin, the Kaiser announced new German military spending; this irritated Churchill, who replied in a belligerent speech in Glasgow two days later. In this impulsive speech, not cleared with Asquith or the Cabinet, Churchill referred to the German navy as a luxury fleet, an expression unhappily more insulting in German than in English. In Germany Churchill was assailed as the overbearing Englishman, and in England as a warmonger, undercutting Haldane's mission. Yet the German government appears to have been committed firmly to its building program, and Churchill's speech did not influence the outcome. Accordingly, when Churchill in March, 1912 introduced his counter building proposals, they called for a 60% superiority over Germany's dreadnought program. Yet he also offered to suspend all shipbuilding for any year that Germany would do the same. Churchill was likely sincere in offering a naval holiday, but the unofficial German reply was discouraging and the initiative was not pursued. Politicians on neither side of the North Sea seemed to realize that the avoidance of conflict must be pursued as vigorously as preparations for the conflict that might come. The anticipation of misfortune can create its own momentum.

Growing concern for security in the North Sea led to reductions in British naval strength in the Mediterranean. The French fleet assumed primary responsibility there, in effect committing Britain to the defense of the French Atlantic coast. The lines between friend and foe were hardening. Accordingly, when Churchill brought in the naval estimates in March, 1913, they amounted to over one million pounds increase above the previous year's estimates, already vast. Churchill renewed his offer of a shipbuilding holiday to Germany, which was spurned there as mere speechmaking designed as a sop to unhappy Liberals. This was not too unfair, for Churchill did not push his proposals past the speech-making stage. Certainly much Liberal opinion was near rebellion when Winston announced in November, 1913 that his March, 1914 estimates would have to go up again. Lloyd George, by then the Chancellor of the Exchequer, was foremost among critics, and objected when Winston indicated he would want a three-million-pound increase. In January, 1914 the conflict between the two most forceful personalities in the Cabinet became so intense that it seemed the Cabinet might smash up. In the end Asquith got Winston's estimates down about a half-million, against the promise of future guarantees of shipbuilding levels that Churchill wanted. The conflict within the Cabinet showed that the traditional Liberal position of economy, isolation, and reform was still powerful within the government down to the eve of war.

Churchill, however, was by now deeply involved in operational planning at the Admiralty in case war came. At the Admiralty, the chief danger to British commerce was seen as coming from surface cruisers. Submarine attacks upon merchantmen without warning were considered unthinkable, and convoying as not worth the nuisance. Churchill and the admirals were at one in these mistaken views. Churchill did push a government war-risks insurance scheme, which was important in keeping shipping moving when war came. The Admiralty did recognize the threat of the torpedo and mine to warships by abandoning a close blockade of the German coast for a distant watch. Churchill, always aggressive, was not very happy about this necessary decision, and drew a sharp comment from Admiral Richmond that merely to steam about the sea is not to take the offensive. This brilliant officer had touched Winston's weakness, his tendency to rush into action with underdeveloped planning. Churchill's personal weakness made the deficiency of an effective planning organization within the Admiralty a critical shortcoming.

For an event that the nations of Europe had insured against, then reinsured, and insured again, World War I came suddenly. The assassination of the heir to the Austro-Hungarian throne in Sarajevo by a Serbian nationalist on June 28, 1914, gradually escalated into a confrontation, with no retreat for Triple Entente and Triple Alliance powers. Churchill had proposed in October, 1913 that the 1914 summer maneuvers be the occasion to test mobilization of the entire Royal Navy, including reserve units. This had been done, and the reserve forces were on the way to demobilization when stopped by Prince Louis, the First Sea Lord, who heard that Serbia had rejected the harsh Austrian demands that had followed upon the assassination of the Archduke Francis Ferdinand. Churchill, who had been home with his wife, confirmed Battenberg's wise precaution and rushed back to the Admiralty. By July 31 the main forces were all at their assigned war stations, and the following day Sir John Jellicoe took command of the Grand Fleet at Scapa Flow. Come what may, the navy was ready.

Not so was the Cabinet. Sir Edward Grey had followed the growing continental crisis without much reference to that body which contained many non-interventionist members, much as he had done in his diplomacy since 1905. As the crisis in Europe grew, so did the Cabinet crisis. There were three groups: the unreserved interventionists, led by Churchill but surely including Asquith and Grey; the fence-sitters, of whom Lloyd George was the most important; and finally those who would resign before they would wage war. In the end these last were only two, Lord Morley and John Burns, who had much support among the Liberal rank and file. The middle group were carried into war by the German violation of Belgian neutrality, guaranteed by Britain.

Already Churchill was acting vigorously. He ordered British forces to follow the powerful German warship *Goeben* in the Mediterranean, pending a formal declaration of war. But the *Goeben* escaped, partly through anxiety not to violate Italy's territorial waters—Italy was expected, rightly, to defect from the Triple Alliance. But poor communications and a less-than-Nelsonic admiral in the Mediterranean also allowed the *Goeben* to reach Constantinople, strengthening the pro-German Turkish leadership who were determined to bring Turkey into the conflict as Germany's ally. Their ultimate success in achieving this goal was serious because it severed the best line of communications between Russia and her two western Entente partners. Churchill, enraged over the *Goeben's* escape, did not forget it.

This was not the only early setback for Churchill. Three cruisers were lost to a single German submarine in the North Sea. Worst of all, a British squadron was outgunned and its chief units sunk in the South Pacific. Public opinion was quick to blame the Admiralty for these setbacks. But more ugly was the outcry against Prince Louis of Battenberg, whose only crime was his German ancestry. The government supinely accepted Battenberg's dignified resignation.

To replace Battenberg, Churchill pressed upon a doubting Asquith for the return of the seventy-four-year-old Admiral Fisher. Churchill got his way and at once collected two dividends. In the first place, Fisher's public popularity and good standing with the Tories eased pressure upon Churchill. Secondly, the old sea-dog, after looking at Churchill's proposals to send ships to seek and destroy the forces of Admiral von Spee which had won the action in the South Pacific, at once upped the forces and packed them off to the South Atlantic. Fisher's thrust was direct on target. Von Spee was caught and annihilated in the battle of the Falklands in early December, 1914. By early 1915 the oceans were everywhere secure for British shipping and the sun shone upon the Admiralty. Yet the conjunction of Churchill and Fisher was a potentially hazardous combination. Beatty correctly predicted that two such strong-willed men would prove one too many for harmony at the Admiralty. A shrewd political observer put the matter succinctly: "Churchill co-opted Fisher to relieve the pressure against himself, but he had no intention of letting anyone else rule the roost. . . . Here, then, were two strong men of incompatible tempers both bent on an autocracy."[3] Admiral Fisher's views are also on record. As the tempestuous First Sea Lord emerged from services at Westminster Abbey, he was heard to mutter: "Resurrected! Resurrected! Resurrected! Again!"[4]

If the Admiralty's problem was two men at the top, the government's problem by early 1915 appeared to be no man at the top. When war came, Asquith did not radically adjust either his Cabinet or his government to meet the new situation. Perhaps, like most men, he expected a short war, similar that of 1870-71. Yet his new War Secretary, Lord Kitchener, had promptly and correctly declared it would be a long war. Kitchener was the Cabinet's notable addition; he brought to it his fame as an imperial soldier and the confidence he inspired, especially among Tories. The Conservatives, however, did not enter a war coalition government, although Bonar Law refrained from criticising government conduct of the war.

The British Cabinet in 1914 had no formal agenda or secretariat, and got military advice only through the two separate service departments. Asquith was accustomed to running the Cabinet as a board-chairman. Leaving the initiative to the most energetic Cabinet members, he adjudicated disagreements and declared judgments in Cabinet meetings. This haphazard approach to waging war turned the Cabinet into a debating arena and left the head of the government without direct professional military advice. By November, 1914 a war council evolved which included the most important ministers and service advisers and a secretary, but it quickly ballooned in membership. It failed to achieve an organization where service staffs would have to examine operations jointly. The war council was still responsible to the Cabinet but neither body met regularly. The result was unregulated initiatives, uncoordinated planning, and diffused responsibility. In this arrangement the personalities of ministers meant much. Kitchener was taciturn, and kept military planning in his own hands, saying little to either his civilian colleagues or to military subordinates. Churchill made up in argument for Kitchener's silence. His fertile imagination produced plans that he energetically pushed forward. The two service ministers did not coordinate their labors, nor did Asquith do it for them.

Initial military events in the West should have flashed warning signals in London that haphazard habits were dangerous in modern war. The British Expeditionary Force had gone to France as long agreed. There it had casually moved forward directly into the path of the main German thrust, a great sweeping movement aiming to cross the Seine below Paris and encircle the French capital. Both British and Germans were startled by meeting the other. The badly shaken British commander, Sir John French, led the "retreat from Mons" in the face of overwhelming German strength. Kitchener himself had to go to the continent to restore his field commander's nerves as Sir John was ready to retreat into

Brittany. Because the German right wing had also lost the decisive energy and tight coordination needed for success, the B.E.F. was able to join French forces in halting German momentum in the "Battle of the Marne." As the front stabilized, each opponent tried to outflank the other, producing the "race to the sea" which carried the front to the coast. The two sides had stumbled into a deadlock.

Churchill had become involved in the land combat. As the B.E.F. recoiled from Mons, it was thought imperative to slow the advance of the German right wing by any expedient. Accordingly Churchill, always ready to act in an emergency, rushed hastily trained naval forces to the ports of Ostend and Dunkirk to create a diversion on the German flank. This brief foray in late August was followed by a longer sortie around Dunkirk in September, with some army forces added. The engagement involved some experiments with scouting vehicles equipped to cross ditches and other barriers to ordinary motor vehicles. Churchill, always enthusiastic about technological innovation, urged on these early experiments with what would evolve into the tank. But the forces could not push forward in the face of vast German strength.

By early October, part of the Belgian army, shoved aside by the German thrust into France, was in serious difficulty around the great port of Antwerp. Neither the French nor the British high command on the continent seemed to have time to spare to consider the Belgian plight or the critical situation along the coast, so again Churchill plunged into action. He rushed a naval brigade to Antwerp and himself followed it on October 3. Once there, Winston proposed to exchange the Admiralty for a field command, which produced gales of laughter in the Cabinet. Only Kitchener seemed to find the proposal reasonable. Asquith told Winston to come home.

Antwerp fell on October 10, and some British forces, withdrawing, were forced into internment in Holland. Churchill was assailed for this, and the usual charge of recklessness leveled at him. Ian Hamilton, a friend of Winston's, but also a professional soldier, described him handling the hastily raised British forces "as if he were Napoleon and they were the Old Guard, flinging them right into the enemy's opening jaws." And Asquith portrayed Winston just back from Antwerp as having "tasted blood" and beginning "like a tiger to raven for more," asking to be relieved of the Admiralty and "put in some kind of military command." Yet he had succeeded in buying vital time by holding up German forces who were distracted from the critical front, and delayed in attacking British and French forces to the south. Churchill's contribution to frustrating the grand German strategy was very real, much more so than that of his critics, whose levity suggests that they were much slower than Churchill to recognize just how serious the situation was. By late October the Western Front had begun to settle down to a slugging match. Gradually, violent direct-encounter battles gave way to trenches, barbed wire, and fixity of position. By the end of November movement had stopped in the West and soon after in the East. The short war most had expected suddenly began to look permanent.

The first to perceive that there was a deadlock, and the first to propose to do something about it, was Churchill. By late 1914 both the French effort at quick victory and the Russian attempt had failed in Lorraine and at Tannenberg respectively, just as the German plan had failed on the Marne. Churchill realized that a new plan was needed. He had a plan, a profound proposal the success or failure of which could be decisive in the long run.

Faced with a stalemate, everyone began looking for the key to victory. For most of the army, the key lay in France, the decisive front where the army was committed. Its leadership demanded every man, every gun, every shell against the main enemy, the German army. The army's argument was persuasive: if the German army in the West was smashed, the war would be won. But there was also a weakness to this argument. The cost, especially in manpower, might become prohibitive. Was there another, cheaper way? Already Churchill believed so. He wished to knock out not the strongest, but the weakest enemy link: Turkey, which had entered the war in October.

From the defeat of the Turk, Churchill hoped for much: communications with Russia restored, Balkan neutrals encouraged to side with the Entente and, hopefully, Italy's alliance also gained. These gains in turn would seal the fate of Austria, assailed from three directions. Then, lastly, an isolated Germany would be confronted with overwhelming power. This was Churchill's theme. In fact, more was at stake than he then recognized. In 1917 a Bolshevik revolution would sweep Russia, carry her out of the war, and establish the giant Communist state that has had so great an impact upon the course of modern world affairs. Much of the foundation of Bolshevik success lay in Russian war

weariness born out of military failure. That failure, in turn, owed more
to a shortage of arms than to any lack of manpower or courage. The
speculation inevitably arises: What might have been the course of
history if Western munitions could have been supplied to Russian
armies, even as late as 1916, when Russia had still been capable of
mounting the great Brusilov offensive? In World War II it would be the
Russian front that absorbed and ultimately destroyed the bulk of the
German army. Might it have been so in World War I? And would a
militarily successful government have fallen to the Bolsheviks? These
were the great, unknown stakes, hidden from view in the future, when
Churchill set his gaze upon the Dardanelles.

These straits, leading from the Aegean to the Sea of Marmara, Constantinople, and through the Bosphorus into the Black Sea, had a long
military history. The north side of the Dardanelles is formed by the
Gallipoli peninsula. As early as the outbreak of war, Churchill had
thought of using a Greek army to attack Gallipoli while a British fleet
assulted the Dardanelles. This was a sound approach, a combined operation, but Greek politics denied Churchill his army. He turned for forces
to Kitchener, who said he could give none.

By January, 1915 the Balkan situation was deteriorating. Not only
had Greece not come in, but Serbia was in trouble and Bulgaria showed
signs of joining the enemy. The hard-pressed Russian command, which
had generously answered frantic Western calls for a premature offensive
in 1914, now begged for a Western effort of any sort against Turkey. In
truth, the Russian crisis was soon over, but it was an ominous warning
for the future. At the time of the crisis, Admiral Fisher, developing a
plan of the war council's secretary, Maurice Hankey, had mentioned
warships forcing the straits in conjunction with land operations on
either side. Churchill, frustrated by his inability to find any land forces
for the operation, wired the British admiral who commanded the forces
off the Dardanelles. Could he use part of Fisher's plan? Force the straits
with ships alone? The Admiralty, said Churchill, would accept heavy
losses if success could be gained. Admiral Carden, a cautious man,
returned a cautious answer indicating that a step-by-step operation,
pounding down the Turkish forts, might succeed. Carden was the re-
cipient of Churchill's swift response, telling him to develop his plans
and state his needs for the operation. Churchill was determined to go
ahead with a purely naval operation, a decision later bitterly criticized,

in view of the traditional advantage forts possessed over warships in combat. Yet this was not to be the real problem that Carden would face.

On January 13, Churchill presented his naval plan to the war council, with the added promise that the *Queen Elizabeth,* the first of the new 15-inch gun battleships, would be sent to bolster the assault. The war council approved the plan. Neither admirals nor Kitchener criticized it. Yet someone should have, for such an operation flew in the face of previous military experience. British empiricism, and Churchill's enthusiasm, had triumphed over careful planning and combined operations. A brilliant strategic concept had been made dependent upon an inadequate operational plan that in essence expected ships to take and hold a peninsula.

Admiral Fisher, now deeply concerned about the possible drain of the Dardanelles operation upon the Grand Fleet at Scapa Flow, met with Asquith and Churchill. His arguments were overwhelmed—not surprisingly, for he had based his legitimate concern upon the wrong premise. The Grand Fleet's margin was ample; the deficiency was with the Dardanelles plan. For his part, Asquith thought that if Carden's attack went badly it could just be broken off. True enough, but then what? On January 28, Fisher was restrained from resigning only by Kitchener's intervention, yet this dramatic episode in the war council did not lead to a reexamination of the problem. Muddling through ruled the day.

The Admiralty was full of worried admirals, but the defective structure there, and Churchill's unwillingness to listen to the junior lords of the Admiralty Board, rendered their concern ineffective. Yet the greatest failure was at the top. Coordination was lacking—if it had been present, it could have led to a combined operation. For the War Office in fact had troops, both ten first-line Territorial Divisions and one regular army division. But Kitchener, despising the Territorials, had pledged the regular army division to the Western Front. The Territorial forces were part of the earlier Haldane reforms; they were a vast improvement in their level of training over the voluntary associations that had preceeded them. Kitchener, who had been out of England for almost forty years prior to 1914, did not recognize this improvement, and placed his faith in new army divisions raised upon volunteer recruitment, for Britain entered World War I without enacting any military service requirement. Kitchener had hoped for 100,000 recruits in the first six months of war; he got 500,000 in the first month and 100,000 more each month for the following eighteen months. This vast outpouring of manpower quite swamped the available training facilities. None of the new army divisions was ready for use in early 1915. But this was not the limit of his forces; there was an Australian-New Zealand army corps (ANZAC) training in Egypt. Kitchener did not move until March 12. He told General Ian Hamilton that he was to command 80,000 men "to support the fleet" at the Dardanelles. This followed Kitchener's promise in February of army support "at a later stage" for the navy. Hamilton's instructions bore this out; he was to follow up a naval victory, or intervene only if the naval effort had reached the last extremity. This by no stretch of the imagination constituted a carefully planned, combined operation. Indeed, Hamilton was given no plan at all. Yet by March 12, Kitchener, too, had been told that combined operations were needed. Not until March 16 did the regular army division begin to leave for the East, in tardy answer to the now-concerned Churchill's mid-February pleas. But Churchill's pleas had been only for forces to reap the fruits of naval victory. Either Churchill was trying to put together a combined operation on the run, or he was becoming shaken by his naval advisers.

Whatever Churchill's February thoughts, the events of early March had put an end to visions of fruits of victory. Carden's attacks of March 10-14 failed because of Turkish minefields, not the forts' guns, and the timid admiral collapsed. His second-in-command, Admiral de Robeck, made a last, grand attempt on March 18, and lost several ships to the mines. On March 22 de Robeck and Hamilton agreed that no purely naval attempt should again be tried. This decision would lead in time to those land operations, the Gallipoli campaign, which would be marked by incredible ineptitude by generals, incredible heroism by the troops so terribly misused, great opportunities lost, and a quarter million casualties sustained.

Yet the naval attack had come within an ace of success. The forts were down to a few shells—which had not been effective anyway; the remaining minefields were not extensive and were vulnerable to proper minesweeping technique. The failure at the Dardanelles in March was a failure of leadership on the part of the admirals and an excessive gentlemanliness in Hamilton, a fault which would cost him much in future land operations.

Churchill's frantic efforts to push de Robeck into another attempt failed. But such frantic appeals would not have been necessary if there had been proper planning at home to begin with. On March 16, 1915, Captain Hankey, reporting on Carden's initial check, wrote Asquith to ask if the war council ought not to ascertain definitely the scope of the operations contemplated at the Dardanelles, and the extent of the preparations needed to carry the operations to success. It is a question no responsible official should have to be asked in the middle of a campaign. Yet when the war council considered Hankey's letter, no action was taken on it. Responsibility for the failure was clearly widely spread, although circumstances would lead to a more narrow allotment of public condemnation, chiefly to Churchill.

On May 15, Fisher resigned as First Sea Lord, on the narrow issue of what naval forces were proper to support the Gallipoli operations, and on the larger issue that the Admiralty was not big enough for two chiefs. Since he could not control Churchill, he would go. The resignation, the end of a long struggle of will and emotion between the two men, came at a time of political crisis. Strenuous efforts were made by Churchill and Asquith to persuade the admiral to return to his post, but without success. Rather, Fisher resorted to methods of intrigue, perhaps in hopes of replacing Churchill, or perhaps out of sheer instability of temperament. In a letter on May 16, Fisher had assured Churchill: "I am sure you know in your heart no one has ever been more faithful to you than I have. . . . " The next day Fisher wrote to Andrew Bonar Law, the Tory leader, that " W.C. MUST go at all costs! . . . W.C. is a bigger danger than the Germans . . .," and he concluded the letter: *"Please burn and don't mention."*[5] This letter moved Bonar Law, already profoundly distrustful of Churchill's judgment, to action. Other aspects of the war's direction had served to intensify Tory discontent with the course of events. A major British offensive in the West had failed, and on May 14, *The Times* had charged that this failure was the consequence of an inadequate supply of artillery shells, thus attacking Kitchener's management of the War Office, and indirectly the government's whole conduct of the war.

On May 19, Asquith announced the formation of a coalition government. Political victory went to Asquith, who survived, to Lloyd George, furious about Kitchener's mismanagement of the War Office, and to the Tories, who entered the government. Churchill lost. He was shunted to the insignificant Duchy of Lancaster, while Balfour took the Admiralty. Considering how the Tories hated him, Churchill was lucky to have anything. Winston continued to press for a continuation of the Gallipoli campaign, but now to an audience made up largely of enemies. Continued misfortune led to withdrawal, completed in early 1916, the only stage of the entire operation that was skillfully executed. An investigation of the whole affair led to a report issued in 1917 placing heavy blame on Churchill. Yet the report was broad in assessing responsibility. Its condemnation of Churchill was mild compared to the attacks made on him by the Tories, and by much public opinion at the time. Terrible condemnations, led by C. E. W. Bean, the Australian official historian and a participant at Gallipoli, summed up the indictment, that through Churchill's "excess of imagination, a layman's ignorance of artillery, and the fatal power of a young enthusiasm to convince older and slower brains, the tragedy of Gallipoli was born"[6] The attacks on Churchill were powered perhaps more by strong emotions than by careful judgment, understandable in view of the horrible casualties the courageous Dominion forces had sustained at Gallipoli. An eye-witness described one Australian attack:

> The enemy's shelling was shifted on to them in one great concentration of hell. The machine-guns bellowed and poured on them sheets of flame and of ragged death, buried them alive. They were disembowelled. Their clothing caught fire, and their flesh hissed and cooked before the burning rags could be torn off or beaten out.[7]

Men who had so suffered and been so terribly misused were understandably quick to center their legitimate grievance upon an identifiable human culprit. Churchill was the most convenient target, and Gallipoli would long continue to haunt his political career, even threatening for a time to destroy it.

Churchill always believed his fault was in having tried to carry out a great operation of war from a position of inadequate authority. There is much to be said for this. But Churchill made neither the best use of the position he occupied, nor of the professional advice available to him. But above all, it was the war council and Britain's system for running the war that were at fault.

The new coalition was not designed to revolutionize the conduct of the war, but only to refurbish the government's public image and rally political support. Kitchener remained at the War Office, increasingly a public image rather than a power in affairs. Much power passed to the energetic Lloyd George, who became head of a new Ministry of Munitions, and who had established relations with the Unionist leader, Bonar Law. Law became Colonial Secretary, but exercised much wider authority. The Labour Party figure, Arthur Henderson, was also brought into the Cabinet to broaden its political base. A Liberal free-trader, McKenna, went to the Treasury, a move that most clearly revealed that politics, not prosecution of the war, was the chief concern in the make-up of the new coalition government. Asquith replaced the war council with the Dardanelles Committee, which not only wound up that unhappy affair in early 1916, but also handled all of British strategy. In short, the organization for conducting the war was not changed—only its name. The decision of this new body to liquidate the Gallipoli position was a final blow to Churchill; his reputation was blasted in public and his policy repudiated by the government. On November 15, 1915, Churchill resigned office and went to France to fight in the trenches.

Notes to Chapter III

[1] Vice-Admiral Sir Peter Gretton, *Former Naval Person* (Cassell, London, 1968), p. 61.

[2] Quoted in *Ibid.*, pp. 87-88.

[3] Lord Beaverbrook, *Politicians and the War* (Collins, London, 1960), p. 98.

[4] Quoted in A. J. Marder, ed., *Fear God and Dread Nought* (Cape, London, 1959), III, 40.

[5] *Ibid.*, pp. 231, 237-238.

[6] Quoted in Robert Rhodes James, *Gallipoli* (Macmillan, New York, 1965), p. 352.

[7] *Ibid.*, p. 154.

CHAPTER FOUR

The Lloyd George Era: 1915–1922

The man who resigned from the government on November 15, 1915 was probably the most distrusted man in England. Churchill believed, and no one contradicted him, that his political career was ruined. He sought the relief of active service and even in this he suffered disappointment. Winston had hoped to get the command of a brigade, but had to settle for the command of a battalion, very nearly an insult, but he took it. The soldiers he commanded remembered him as a capable, conscientious, and concerned officer. He left behind him in London a strong plea that the government adopt conscription, for Britain was still waging a world war with volunteers only. Churchill was thus consistent in his belief that war could not be won by half-measures, or by half-hearted men. Conscription went against the libertarian tradition of the Liberal Party. That the Tory members of Asquith's coalition government wished it made conscription even less palatable to the Liberal remnant, excluding Lloyd George. For David Lloyd George was rapidly becoming a power, if not a party, unto himself. He had been instrumental in forcing the coalition upon Asquith. He had new ties to the Tories, especially to their leader, Bonar Law, and he had old ties to radical, democratic Britain. Like Churchill, Lloyd George did not believe in half-measures, and had all but seized munitions production from the palsied hand of that fading giant, now more reputation than man, Lord Kitchener.

The whole Dardanelles affair had been a plan, an attempt, to find a way to win the war. This momentous question still confronted the coalition government. In fact, the British government was tied by its pre-war plan to align its army with France's. The German penetration onto French soil riveted French attention to the Western Front; so, too, it worked to rivet the British army there. Churchill and Hankey had both cautioned that the Western Front was not promising; barbed wire, machine-guns, vast artillery, trenches dug in series, and the soon ever-present mud gave defense a heavy advantage over offense. But the army high command believed that yet more artillery could pound down the enemy front, that German troops would be "used up" in infantry encounter, and ultimate breakthrough achieved.

A crucial problem faced the army leaders: attack tended to use up more of the attacking than of the defending troops. The government, without an alternative to the generals' plan, accepted it. If 1915 had been the year of amateurs and their Dardanelles escapade, then 1916 would be the year of the professionals. And no soldier was more professional than Sir Douglas Haig, who became Commander-in-Chief of the British armies in France on December 19, 1915. At much the same time Sir William Robertson, a remarkable general who had risen from the ranks, returned from France to become Chief of the Imperial General Staff, with authority, gained at the fading Kitchener's expense, to advise the government in military matters. The always hopeful, greatly determined and tenacious Haig, and the taciturn, blunt Robertson combined to give forceful representation to the advocates of an all-out effort on the Western Front. No one in the government was prepared to deny the generals their demands, or in return demand an explanation of how the generals' tactical concepts could produce the decisive breakthrough that the generals always expected after just one more push, just one more assault.

A war of attrition had its fascination for German commanders, too, and a long, bitter struggle around the exposed French position at Verdun had opened the 1916 campaigning season. While French and Germans bled and died around Verdun—the French dying more, as the Germans had intended (yet not enough more)—the Russians had launched the great Brusilov offensive in the East. It did well initially, and soon the Italians, who had joined the Entente in 1915, launched their own attacks against Austria. This left Britain the decisive role; it was her forces who were to deliver the knock-out blow.

At the end of May, 1916 there opened in the North Sea off the coast of Jutland the long-awaited encounter between Jellicoe's Grand Fleet and the German High Seas Fleet. The result was vastly disappointing to a British nation nurtured upon the tradition of Nelson at the Nile, Copenhagen, and Trafalgar. Unlike Nelson's triumphs, Jutland was not a crushing defeat for the enemy. Indeed, the battle, really a succession of encounters under deteriorating conditions of visibility, was to all appearances indecisive. The British had actually lost more ships, although it was the Germans who broke off the main action and ran for harbor. The High Seas Fleet never came out again; Germany would turn to the submarine to seek victory at sea; she would fight not against battleships, but against merchant ships. This was not clear to the discontented British public or to the British admirals, who did not adjust their strategy. Indeed Jellicoe convinced himself that the German turn away had been a ploy to lure him into a submarine ambush. He refused to risk his battleships south of the latitude of Scotland and clamored for destroyers, which were soon to be far more desperately needed by the naked merchant ships.

The British public sustained yet another blow with the death of Lord Kitchener, who had retained his immense popularity with the uninformed man in the street. On June 5 he drowned when making a journey to Russia, a government tactic to get him temporarily out of England. Yet his death had the effect of revealing just how naked the government, without a victory anywhere, looked by mid-1916. Lloyd George, the most energetic man in the government, became the new Secretary of State for War. Never was a stage so dramatically set for the army. Everyone now awaited Sir Douglas Haig's decisive blow in the West.

On July 1, 1916 Haig launched his great offensive in the Somme

River region which gives its name to the campaign now opening. By nightfall the results were clear: there was virtually no gain, and certainly no breakthrough. Some 57,000 casualties had been sustained, 60% of the officers and 40% of the men engaged in the assault—the worst day in the history of the British army. Yet the offensive went on, never so ambitiously again, into November. The generals' strategy had failed to achieve decisive victory, although the German forces were terribly punished. As the forces on the Western Front were constituted in 1916, there was little chance of decisive success. In this the generals' strategy differed from Churchill's strategy at the Dardanelles, where opportunity for success was repeatedly bungled away by inadequate planning, incapable naval commanders, and finally colossal military blunders. Long into the Somme campaign the generals possessed the entire support of the Minister of War. David Lloyd George was tied to Robertson and Haig in his determination to wage all-out war, to deliver the knock-out blow, a view he publically proclaimed as late as September, 1916. When the Somme campaign was finally closed down, and the casualties totaled up, the British Army had sustained 498,054 dead, wounded and missing. Of these, 115,364 were dead. The knock-out blow had not been delivered. Haig was disappointed, but not discouraged, for he knew he had hurt the German army badly; he was convinced that, if he continued to pound away, victory would be his—as indeed it ultimately was. But the British public and politicians did not see the wounds inflicted upon the German Army so clearly as they saw the fearful British casualty toll. It was a moot point if Haig could secure victory before his casualty figures became intolerable to a democratic public and their elected politicians.

The public was now restless, the newspapers savage toward the government, and the Conservative backbenchers on the verge of revolt. This convinced Bonar Law in early November that he would have to do something. By the same time, Lloyd George at the War Office became convinced that, since his generals had not found a quick way to deliver the knock-out blow, he would have to. When President Wilson earlier had hinted at a negotiated peace, it was Lloyd George who had proclaimed no compromise. A former Canadian of talent and ambition, Max Aitken, then a rising newspaper publisher and soon to become Lord Beaverbrook, was instrumental in joining Tory discontent, an unhappy Law, and a restless, determined Lloyd George into a coordinated effort to revamp the direction of the war at the top. Asquith resisted the proposed changes that would reduce him to a figurehead. Lloyd George won the struggle. The Liberals were variously discontented, too. About half of them followed Lloyd George, as did most of Labour, and finally the Tories, not all enthusiastically. Given the deep antagonisms still festering from pre-war conflict, the strains of war, and the brutal political in-fighting, Lloyd George's feat in getting together an adequate base of support for his leadership was a triumph of political skill. On December 6, 1916, he became Prime Minister.

The great Jacobin had seized the first power in the State. The responsibilities of the first place in the State had seized him; never again were any words about "knock-out blows" heard from the lips of David Lloyd George. A five-man War Cabinet was set up, with only Law as Chancellor of the Exchequer—he was also Leader of the Commons—responsible for a department. Two great Tory proconsuls, Lords Curzon and Milner, accustomed to strong executive authority from their experiences in India and South Africa respectively, came in with the Labour leader, Arthur Henderson. Henderson was included for national unity, and largely ignored by the other four. Lloyd George set up a Cabinet secretariat with Maurice Hankey as secretary to the Cabinet. Lloyd George also brought businessmen into the government, an action viewed at the time as a progressive step to gain efficiency. Some, like Sir Joseph Maclay in Shipping and Sir Auckland Geddes in National Service, were indeed able. Beaverbrook became Minister of Information. Lord Northcliffe, most powerful and least stable of the Press Lords, was soon packed off to the U.S., where he was less dangerous.

Lloyd George wanted to win the war, but without another Somme. He lacked the creative imagination of Churchill but possessed far greater skill in manipulating the pieces already on the playing board. As he could not have Churchill—the Tories would come into his coalition only if Winston were kept out—he had recourse to finding a way around to victory with the tools available. These were not very encouraging. The most dangerous of the Tory backbenchers, Sir Edward Carson, went to the Admiralty when Balfour became Lloyd George's Foreign Secretary. Carson's policy was to serve the admirals. But the admirals, especially Jellicoe who became First Sea Lord in December, needed to be forced to think, not insulated from criticism. The Tory Lord Derby, a popular weakling who became War Minister, was the servant of the generals. Just as Lloyd George had come to doubt the capabilities of the military, so they had little confidence in him, and less understanding of the burdens of democratic political leadership. The two service ministers did not close this gap. The generals could not make their views clear to the critical Prime Minister; he in turn over-powered them in debate and sent them away discontented. They chose to say little to him about their war and he did not consult them as he planned his war. The essential unity at the top needed to prosecute modern war thus was not achieved.

The year 1917 was bleak. In February the Germans opted for unlimited submarine warfare, risking American intervention against the hope of starving out Britain. It was a gamble the Germans nearly won. The United States declared war in April while an hysterical Admiralty told the government that they could not control shipping losses. Jellicoe insisted that the army must win the war at once or the struggle could not go on. Effective convoy escort he declared unworkable. Fortunately, shipping officials and junior officers in the Admiralty's Trade Division knew better, and leaked information to Lloyd George. Carson and Jellicoe fought tenaciously, but the threat of Lloyd George coming to preside himself at the Admiralty was too much for them; convoying was tried. Thus at the eleventh hour Britain was saved from the admirals; the people would not starve. As quickly as was decent, Sir Eric Geddes replaced Carson and Admiral Wemyss, a genial openminded man, became First Sea Lord.

If Britain had been saved from the admirals, could her manhood be saved from the generals? Lloyd George was determined to try. Already the generals had gained much from the nation. Conscription had been carried through in 1916. Lloyd George had set up what was virtually national service, military or industrial, for all able-bodied men. Lloyd George distrusted his own generals' plans; his problem was that he did not himself have a plan, but only a method—the search for a way around. The Salonika front, long stalled in Greece, seemed briefly to beckon. But it was a way around that led nowhere, for the key to success in the East was Russia, and in 1917 Russia fell out of the war. The Tsarist regime was in full collapse from ineptitude, military failure, and the great burdens the Russians had carried. Yet even before Russia fell out, Lloyd George had found a general with a plan—a French general, the articulate and English-speaking General Nivelle. He had come to London to present a full plan of campaign to the British War Cabinet. The plan impressed Lloyd George, but in reality it was only a variation upon the old chimera of a breakthrough. But Lloyd George had his own ax to grind, anyway. It would be chiefly a French effort, and would tie Haig to French orders, Lloyd George hoped. The Nivelle offensive failed as Haig had correctly foreseen. The pity was that Haig could not convey the conclusions of his cool intelligence to his own political leader. The failure of Nivelle in turn brought mutinies in the French Army at a time when widespread war weariness and socialist agitation for a new order were alike rising. A frightened French government installed General Pétain to restore morale and discipline, but any serious fighting in the West would have to be done by Haig. Jellicoe was clamoring for just this at the time, calling for Haig to take submarine bases along the Channel before the war at sea was lost.

One man opposed a new British offensive. In a secret session on May 10, 1917, Churchill, who had returned from the front, rose in the Commons to argue for only an active position of defense in the West until the Americans could arrive. So powerful and impressive was Churchill's presentation that Lloyd George was prepared to brave Tory wrath to bring him into the government. In mid-July Churchill went to the Ministry of Munitions. Lloyd George managed to ride out a violent Tory reaction, with over 100 Conservative M. P.'s signing a resolution against the appointment. They still hated Churchill for the Ulster "pogrom," yet more deeply for something more. Churchill did not fit. His extraordinary force and energy, his intense emotions and overpowering rhetoric, in debate or conversation, his political waywardness and seeming instability, turned Churchill in the eyes of these ordinary, conventional men into a great dreadnought run amok in a harbor crowded with fragile-hulled vessels. They hated Churchill most because they feared him and did not understand him.

Churchill at once gripped his new job. He carried through Parliament a Munitions of War Act enabling the government to deal more effectively with growing grievances among the workers. Substantial wage increases were approved. Yet when new labor unrest occurred in 1918, Winston abandoned conciliation and talked about drafting strikers into the army, a proposal which Lloyd George wisely quashed. The Labour leadership, however, seemed to be getting a better understanding of Winston's temperament. Arthur Greenwood observed, more in sorrow than in anger, that "Winston is in one of his Napoleonic moods." Greenwood was close to the key to controlling Churchill: recognition of Winston's basic humanity and the need to argue him out of his more flamboyant inspirations which ran against his own fundamental values of life.

Lloyd George did not have confidence in his generals; however, the Tory backbenchers (who were the core of the government's majority in the Commons), the King, Lord Northcliffe, and much of the public did. Since Lloyd George could not sack his generals he tried to tie their hands by unity of allied command, in itself a sound principle. Nivelle's failure, however, had checked the Prime Minister's initiative here, as had Robertson's vehemently silent opposition. When Haig proposed to strike through Flanders toward the Channel ports, Lloyd George bluntly told his field commander in June, 1917 that he had no faith in the offensive. Yet he and the War Cabinet, yielding to Jellicoe's fears and Haig's optimism, authorized the Flanders offensive. For the government, it was an offensive of desperation that began on July 31, 1917.

In August the rains came, and continued to come, heavier than usual for Flanders in the autumn. Artillery smashed the land's drainage systems. Mud developed on a scale remarkable even to the Western Front; pack animals and in some cases even wounded men were swallowed by the glutinous, ever-present, all-consuming mud. Around the town of Passchendaele men died and drowned in mud.

At the end of November, Haig called off the offensive: disaster in Italy required British aid. The Italian defeat at Caporetto produced hurried French and British assistance and provided Lloyd George with a golden opportunity for unified command. Robertson balked, but times had changed. Haig's failure in Flanders had pushed important people in London over to the Prime Minister's camp, however reluctantly. Generals were even being criticized in the newspapers. Misfortune rained down. A successful tank attack at Cambrai was thrown away when a German counterattack caught the British Army unawares. In December, 1917 the new Bolshevik government in Russia negotiated an armistice, freeing German manpower for the West. Several of Haig's chief staff officers were now sacked. The Prime Minister determined to restrain Haig by holding reserves in England. He also hoped to create a general reserve in France which a Supreme War Council would control, not Haig. By February, 1918 the Prime Minister felt strong enough at last to replace Robertson with the more flexible Sir Henry Wilson as Chief of the Imperial General Staff. A month later the Germans began their great offensive in the West. Military crisis created the need for an allied commander-in-chief, the French General Foch. The front was stabilized, with everyone, French and British, soldiers and civilians, pulling together—at last.

Even as unity was being so painfully achieved, a final discordant note was struck when on May 7, 1918 a high Tory paper published the charges of General Sir Frederick Maurice that the government had lied to the House of Commons in denying that Haig's fighting strength had not been diminished prior to the German spring offensives. In a debate two days later, Lloyd George skillfully managed to demonstrate that the government's manpower figures had come from Maurice's own office in the War Department. Asquith's motion for a Select Committee investigation was then defeated, 293 to 106. Whatever the truth about the manpower, and Maurice had certainly bungled a potentially damaging charge, the debate and vote revealed that the government was in control of the House of Commons and could act strongly. The crisis in the West produced 650,000 new troops for Haig between March and August. American troops were flowing in. Foch launched a successful counter-attack on July 18. In August began a general offensive all along the line.

On September 15 the old Salonika front, scene of perpetual inactivity, came to life and by the end of the month Bulgaria had collapsed. General Allenby in Palestine was driving north as the Salonika troops pushed east for Constantinople. On October 4, the German government asked President Wilson for an armistice. On November 9 the Kaiser fled to Holland and two days later the Allies granted the new German Republic an armistice.

World War I cost the British Empire 947,000 dead, of whom 755,000 were from the home islands. Influenza struck an exhausted people in the terrible winter of 1918-19 and claimed 150,000 more lives. Britain had poured out millions of treasure to her allies and had borrowed millions from America. Hundreds of millions of overseas investments had been liquidated. The Russian debt was irrecoverable; so would others be, but the Americans would demand repayment. Britain's industrial equipment had been run hard for several years, and domestic wear and tear needed to be made good. No one doubted it would be. No one doubted that the terrible blood sacrifice would be honored in a better, greater post-war Britain. The night of November 11, Lloyd George and Churchill dined alone at Downing Street. Churchill recalled that the walls were hung with portraits of Nelson and Wellington, and perhaps not inappropriately, George Washington. Would the British statesmen be as successful in carrying their country from war to peace as the father of the American Republic had been?

Churchill would waste no time trying. Before dinner he had met with his Munitions staff to initiate conversion to peace. Lloyd George was anxious for an election that would ratify victory in war and provide a mandate for peace negotiations. Churchill agreed. He wrote that he was anxious to leave the terrible pre-war party quarrels behind and fight a coalition election. The test of coalition loyalty was basically, although not entirely, the vote in the Commons' division that followed the debate upon General Maurice's charges. A letter signed by Lloyd George and Bonar Law—called a "coupon" by Asquith—endorsed the chosen coalition candidates. Labour ran as an entirely independent party and for the first time on a Socialist program. The campaign in the coupon election brought little honor to anyone. Popular frenzy for revenge upon Germany raged, and the worst political demogogues stoked the fires. Lloyd George, Law, and Churchill all knew the impossibility of the demands. Churchill, under considerable pressure in Dundee, refused to budge from an indemnity claim upon Germany thought economically feasible by a Treasury Committee headed by J. M. Keynes. Yet he admitted that he "dressed it up as well as possible." Under pressure, Lloyd George's claims upon Germany rose, but he also stressed a domestic program, the need to create "a fit country for heroes."

The coalition won nearly 48% of the vote and 478 seats, 355 of them Unionist. Another 48 Tories who lacked the coupon also won. Asquith Liberals got 12% of the vote and 28 seats. Labour polled 22% and gained 63 seats. Asquith himself and Labour pacifists like Ramsay MacDonald were defeated. There were only 7 Irish in the Commons, for 73 Sinn Fein party candidates refused to acknowledge that the Imperial Parliament could rule Ireland, and they met in Dublin. A careful Tory, Stanley Baldwin, called the new Commons at Westminster a lot of hard-faced men who looked as if they had done well out of the war. Most certainly they lacked Baldwin's own generous sense of public service. Lloyd George's peacetime administration left Balfour at the Foreign Office, but Bonar Law became Lord Privy Seal, which relieved him of departmental labors to concentrate upon politics in the Commons. Churchill became Secretary of State for War and Air. His old Tory friend, F. E. Smith, became Lord Chancellor as Lord Birkenhead.

Churchill at once faced a demobilization crisis. A scheme had been started whereby key men needed in converting the economy to peacetime were to be released first. However, because of their essential skills, these were often the last drafted. Despite the scheme being sane economically, it lacked equity. Slow demobilization procedures added to this inequity, and disorders in the army followed. Churchill acted energetically. He at once set up the basic rule of first in, first out, with immediate discharges for men with three or more combat wounds. He upped the rate of release from the army to 10,000 a day, all the transport and processing facilities could handle. It was an impressive display of Churchill in action. He diligently labored to build up good will in the Commons. In Cabinet he argued for a larger budget, especially for air, with little success. Relations inside the Cabinet were not smooth, and on one occasion, Bonar Law, who detested him, suggested Churchill resign. Perhaps because of these internal Cabinet difficulties, Churchill's tenure at War and Air was not entirely happy, and British aviation, in particular, suffered.

No subject so concerned Churchill at the war's end as did Russia. Part of the Bolshevik program had been peace, and upon seizing power the new regime approached Germany, finally concluding a highly unfavorable peace at Brest- Litovsk. The shocked Western Entente powers, especially Britain, were prepared to resort to military intervention in Russia to keep Germany tied down there. Bolshevik power and Russian war-weariness were alike underestimated. Early plans for intervention seemed based upon the idea that neither Russian government nor people need be consulted. Japanese troops, to cite only one wild example, were to be transported across Siberia to fight Germany in European Russia. Some British imperialists were not adverse to seeing what could be grabbed in the Russian Caucasus, particularly the Baku oil fields. To support White Russian forces against the Red Army, British troops were sent to Archangel, where there were stores of British munitions, originally shipped for the effort against Germany. French troops landed at Odessa on the Black Sea. Czech forces in

Siberia were enlisted against the Reds. The U.S. was urged to send forces to the Pacific port of Vladivostok.

These actions, largely based upon emotional reaction to Brest-Litovsk, plus no little fear of Bolshevism, were both disjointed and impractical. The Japanese had no intention of pulling European chestnuts out of the fire; they had their own Asian ambitions to serve. The American government was most cautious about the whole idea of intervention. The Czechs would not fight for the White Russian commander in Siberia, Admiral Kolchak.

This was roughly the situation when Churchill became War Minister. What had begun as an anti-German operation was well on the way to becoming an anti-Bolshevik intervention. At no time was it a practical intervention, yet Churchill would labor to make it so. He failed, for all sorts of reasons: Lloyd George and Woodrow Wilson's realistic caution, universal war-weariness, lack of unified allied goals and programs, White Russian ineptitude, Russian patriotism, and Bolshevik ability. Within the British government there were two anti-Russian themes: fear of a great Russian power astride Britain's imperial possessions in the Persian Gulf and India, and fear of a Bolshevik state that might export revolution, just as Burke had once feared from a Jacobin France.

Churchill correctly recognized that the present allied program of intervention was fatuous. He wanted a much greater effort. Lloyd George balked, correctly reading British war-weariness. Churchill argued that the Bolsheviks represented only themselves, and would lose popular elections held under allied auspices, but he never found a way to secure allied control of Russia for such purposes. In truth, given affairs as constituted in 1919, there was no way. All Churchill's anti-Bolshevik effort accomplished was to antagonize Lloyd George and the Labour Party. Labour's position was influential in restraining British aid to Poland, which had become involved in the war with the Bolsheviks. This conflict was settled in March of 1921. By then the last allied forces (except the Japanese) were out of Russia. Churchill's effort had lost all down the line. He never had much support for his bold policy in the Cabinet; his allies had been coalition backbenchers of the most conservative hue who hated Bolshevism but who did not have to stare practical realities in the face. Churchill was perhaps becoming a threat to his own Prime Minister from the Right. It was essentially a position he would occupy down until the late 1930s and goes far to explain why the Left so distrusted him in those years.

Yet if the tools to accomplish Churchill's foreign policy were never present, the policy itself was not without merit. It was based upon Churchill's belief that an ambitious Japan, and particularly an unstable and unsatisfied Germany, were dangerous forces to world stability. In such an event, he wanted a Russia friendly to Britain. But he did not seem to believe that could be a Bolshevik Russia. He believed a Bolshevik Russia meant a "great Russian" policy, perilous to British Asia. At the same time, he despised the Bolshevik approach to government and society as inhuman. The Bolshevik government, for its part, did not forget the allied intervention. The Soviets blamed the terrible civil war (which they won), and the struggle with Poland, in large part upon the intervention. It was a hardened regime that emerged in Russia by 1922. It had won power by ability, ruthlessness and popularity, and it was determined to hold in an iron grip what it had secured at great cost. Great visions of world revolution would have to wait until Russia was strong and secure. The failure of the Communist ideological offensive of 1919-1921 in Europe had demonstrated that even so unhappy and unstable a land as Germany could not yet be gained. What Churchill feared most had come to be. Both Russia and Germany were hostile to Britain. To the hostility of the former, Churchill had himself contributed much. The long term consequences would be terrible.

German disaffection was assured by the Versailles Treaty. In November, 1918, the moral courage of the German army command and the Kaiser alike had failed. The Kaiser fled into exile, and the high command dumped the broken pieces of their military policy into the hands of a republic rushed into existence to get an armistice from President Wilson. The German people had suffered considerable deprivation from the British blockade but the armistice was a shock, for their army appeared triumphant in the East and still unbowed in the West. Because the high command had no intention of owning up to the responsibility for defeat, a scapegoat was needed. Most available was the new republic centered not in Prussian Berlin but in Goethe's Rhineland home of Weimar. This unfortunate government had to sign a peace treaty with the Allies at Versailles. The price was high. Wilson wanted his 14 Points for world peace, notably a world organization, but could not close the door to his associates' claims either. Lloyd George wanted security for the British Empire, which meant a secure Europe, preferably by means of a not discontented Germany. France wanted security in Europe, by arrangements that would assure a discontented Germany. Italy wanted all it could get.

Inevitably, no one got what he wanted. Italy, whose claims were chiefly upon the old Austrian and Turkish empires, was frustrated by Wilson's doctrine of self-determination of national groups, and emerged into the 1920s as a discontented power. France got Alsace-Lorraine, the Saar for a term of years, and a demilitarized Rhineland, but still did not have the certain security she craved, and tended to blame the Anglo-Saxon Powers for this. They promised France a joint guarantee against unprovoked German aggression. Further, the Allies would keep forces in the Rhineland area for terms of years. Germany was to acknowledge "war guilt," that is, to accept responsibility for all Allied war losses and damages, and thus the burden of paying reparations, the scale of which was left to a future commission to determine. The German army was limited to 100,000 men; tanks, submarines and military aircraft were forbidden. At Paris everyone lost, but President Wilson lost most, for he gave up his status as prophet of a new and better world and became just another money-changer in the temple of great power brokerage at Versailles; what alternative he had is much disputed. He did get the League of Nations, but not for America, for his political enemies at home blocked American entry. The New World had failed to redress the balance of the Old, so a new balance had to be struck in blood payment twenty years later.

Lloyd George, the most dexterous of negotiators, did not come away empty-handed. The German fleet went to Scapa Flow, where it scuttled itself. Wilson did not press "freedom of the seas" upon the British Empire. Throughout, Lloyd George was concerned to get a stable European balance that would leave Britain free to pursue internal reconstruction and imperial consolidation. He had been skillful in his efforts to conciliate the harsh and encourage the moderates. But the end results were disappointing; the French were insecure and the Germans unreconciled. Germany signed the Versailles Treaty, but never accepted it. Yet it is not likely any treaty would have reconciled Germany, for basically what Germans did not accept was the reality of their defeat.

Churchill himself was only obliquely concerned with the peace settlement, but he held strong views about it. He saw the central problem of the peace in the disproportion of national strength between France and Germany. He noted that by 1940 Germany would have twice as many men of military age as France. Winston wished the Cabinet to give France a pledge that Britain would guarantee her security, in exchange for France moderating her settlement demands on Germany, which Churchill believed were sure to aggrieve the Germans. He hoped to conciliate Germany and thus offset his failure to bring down the Bolsheviks in Russia. Churchill dreaded a world with both Germany and Russia alienated from the main world community. He predicted that another war, given the onward movement of technology, would be yet more terrible than the conflict just ended.

Churchill was not alone in his concern. Late in 1919 the brilliant economist, J. M. Keynes, published *The Economic Consequences of the Peace,* in which he argued that the economics terms worked against a prosperous and stable Europe. Keynes' arguments would be challenged later, but they had much influence, helping convince many people that Germany had been unjustly treated and was entitled to a revision of the Versailles settlement. In 1921 the reparation commission set $33,000,000,000 as the sum due from Germany. She was by then already in arrears on initial payments. This started a vicious circle: France and Belgium wanted the reparations before they repaid British war debts; Britain wished this income to pay what it owed the United States; the American government insisted its war loans be repaid, without regard to reparations. As a consequence, everyone nourished a grievance. In the early 1920s Britain negotiated the debt to the U.S. on 62-year terms at an average 3-1/3% interest, but felt badly used by Americans. Even more certain to embitter relations, early in 1923 France occupied the Ruhr when Germany defaulted on some lumber and coal deliveries. Britain objected to this action. Thus the Western nations were divided in policy; Germany, Russia, and Italy all nourished grievances; eastern Europe was an area of new, unstable nations created out of the Austrian, Russian, and Turkish Empires; and the United States demanded its economic due without being willing to shoulder any responsibility in the world community. International anarchy is a fit description of such a world order—or disorder.

The rejection of the Treaty and League of Nations by the United

States Senate, and the rejection of the joint Anglo-American guarantee of France's border with Germany, were most unfortunate, and played a major role in the French government's determination to seek security for itself. Hence the Ruhr occupation of 1923. France also concluded alliances with Poland, Czechoslovakia, Rumania, and Yugoslavia, the first two of which would take on critical significance in the late 1930s. The League of Nations, Woodrow Wilson's bright torch of hope for a better world, flickered fitfully in the dark night of international anarchy, swept by gusts of national antagonism and drenched in downpours of human fears and hatreds. The League lived only from 1920 to 1939, although not officially pronounced dead until 1946. Churchill had warned in 1918 that the League could work only if the great powers were united in using it. Of these, it fell to a disunited Britain and France to carry the burden of making it work, a hopeless task from the first. Italy and Japan sought largely self-interest inside the League; Germany did not enter until 1926, Russia only in 1934, and the U.S. never. The means available to the League for the restraint of arbitrary action by a great power were too weak to be effective. Every nation was in effect free to pursue its own interests to the limits of its own power, for better or worse.

For Britain, almost any change in the world order was apt to be for the worse. She had defended her interests successfully in 1914-18 and had acquired territory in Africa and the Middle East under terms of mandates set up by the League of Nations as a compromise between Wilsonian idealism and European colonial tradition. But by the early 1920s it would be hard to say that Britain was on good terms with any world power. By the same time Japan and the U.S. had clashed over the balance of power in the Far East; both had ambitious naval building programs. These directly threatened the superiority of the Royal Navy, the instrument by which Britain hoped to assure her imperial position. Britain still had a Japanese alliance, certain to antagonize Washington and perhaps not in Britain's long-range interest. In Cabinet debate, Churchill stressed that there could be no policy so fatal to Britain as joining with Japan against the United States. Lloyd George, however, feared British dependence upon the U.S. as even worse.

The force of economic realities and political developments alike favored Churchill's position over Lloyd Geroge's. In 1921 the government decided to concentrate its naval strength in European waters, allowing the Japanese treaty to lapse, and building up Singapore as the base for whatever naval strength could be spared for the Pacific and Indian Oceans. Because the naval force available for Singapore seemed slight, British interests in the Pacific, not to mention Australia and New Zealand, became dependent upon American power. In fact, the two Pacific dominions, as well as Canada, were themselves moving toward reliance upon American strength. The British Empire, willingly or otherwise, was being handed over to Washington's keeping, whether the Americans wanted it or not. This meant, ultimately, the end of that Empire. The events of the 1940s would only complete and ratify what began in the 1920s.

After World War I such international trends were little noticed by the British public, awaiting the land fit for heroes that Lloyd George had promised them. Wartime controls on the economy were ended, then an abrupt price inflation swiftly outran wages. Labor unrest soon followed, with the coal miners the most unhappy. The ancient coal industry was by 1919 in such disarray that Hercules himself might have blanched at cleaning such an Augean Stable. Lloyd George limited himself to a superficial sweeping. A commission led by Mr. Justice Sankey produced no less than four differing reports in 1919 on what to do. Lloyd George picked his way through these alternatives, rejecting nationalization of the industry, but maintaining existing wages while legislating a seven-hour day for the workers. Both owners and miners grudgingly accepted these terms. Events favored the owners; unemployment throughout the economy began to rise frighteningly, doubling between December 1920 and March 1921. By that summer it hit 2,000,000. Thus when the coal mine owners cut wages in 1921, the unions were ill-placed to resist. The miners called upon their reluctant allies, the transport and railway workers, for sympathy strikes. Because such action would coerce the government more than the mine owners, for not they but the public would suffer from the sympathy strikes, the unions' leadership wanted no such showdown. On April 15, 1920—"Black Friday"—they told the miners they would not go out in something akin to a general strike. The miners went back only in July, largely upon the owners' terms. Everyone had cause for bitterness; most blamed the government. In fact, the French occupation of the Ruhr improved overseas markets for British coal, but its benefit came too late to save Lloyd George. As post-war disillusionment set in, the coalition government declined in popularity with its own members and in public support.

In February of 1921 Churchill moved from the War Office to the Colonial Office, thus intensifying his deep involvement in the Irish question. World War I had led to Irish Home Rule becoming law, with its operation temporarily suspended. Military conscription had not been applied in Ireland. But extremists there, working through Sir Roger Casement, sought German aid for their ambition of creating a self-governing Ireland. Casement was captured upon landing in Ireland; he had no German aid to bring anyway. The radicals went ahead alone and rose in Dublin on Easter Monday, 1916, and proclaimed the Irish Republic. It had little public support, and British troops had complete control in four days. Then the British command executed the rebel leaders, while arresting hundreds of Irish. The radical cause had gained its martyrs.

Among Irish radical opinion the strongest party was the Sinn Fein led by Arthur Griffith and Eamon de Valera. In the 1918 election, Sinn Fein swept Ireland outside Ulster; it won 73 seats, against 25 Unionist seats and only 7 of the old Nationalist Home Rulers. The 73 refused to sit at Westminster, but met in Dublin as an Irish Parliament, the Dail Eireann. As such they announced Ireland's independence as a republic on January 21, 1919. Southern Irish Volunteers were transformed into the Irish Republican Army (I.R.A.), commanded by the able and ruthless Michael Collins. He lacked de Valera's political skill, but it was his forceful direction of the Republicans' ambitions that perhaps entitles him to be regarded more than any other man as creator of the Irish Free State. Yet it was de Valera, now free from British imprisonment (which was a distinction many modern national leaders would come to share), who was elected president of the Dail. He set up his own government. There were now two governments in Ireland, Imperial and Sinn Fein. Gradually a civil war developed, with the I.R.A. using guerrilla tactics against British forces. The British government reinforced the over-burdened Royal Irish Constabulary with auxiliary forces, not always under effective political control. The result was a conflict between two largely irresponsible military forces. Atrocities mounted throughout 1920. The policy of the government was attacked by Henderson for Labour and Asquith for the Liberals as "despotic" and "a disgrace to the human race." This was the situation Churchill faced as Colonial Secretary.

Both he and Lloyd George wanted a settlement; indeed, Churchill was prepared to offer a generous measure of Irish self-government. But he characteristically wished to negotiate from strength. In May, 1921 he accepted the need for negotiations. The truce was secured in July, following a dramatic appeal for conciliation by the King in a Belfast speech. The actual negotiations were hard. Formal agreement was achieved only by threats of naked force from Lloyd George and his colleagues. The Irish Treaty of December, 1921 left Ulster part of the United Kingdom and Ireland part of the Empire. The Ulster Unionists, led by Sir James Craig, accepted certain control of Ulster in exchange for abandoning Unionists in the rest of Ireland. Much more critical was the Irish Republican position. Griffith and Collins, who led the negotiations, finally accepted Lloyd George's terms in exchange for practical self-government for the Irish Free State, enjoying the same constitutional status as Canada. Britain would be allowed to keep naval bases in some Irish ports. The Ulster boundary would be re-adjusted by a commission, hopefully in the Free State's decisive favor.

But the Dail split on the treaty. Its membership, reconstituted and expanded in 1921, voted 64 for Griffith, Collins and peace, and 57 for de Valera and what must be war. More serious to the Irish cause, the I.R.A. also divided. Elections in June, 1922 gave the Free state government 58 seats and de Valera's opposition party 35 seats. Civil war was shortly after set off by extremists in Dublin. A peace of exhaustion settled over the Free State in mid-1923. By then Collins was dead by assassination and Griffith of a heart attack.

Churchill's role in these affairs was two-fold: to steer the Treaty through Parliament, and to get both Ulster and the Free State to act with restraint on their border pending the report of the Irish Boundary Commission. Neither was easy. There was much Conservative hostility to the Treaty, but Churchill's great energy led it through the House. Similarly, he labored to get Craig and Collins to keep peace on their uneasy border, a goal somewhat imperfectly achieved. In 1925 the Boundary Commission's report was buried by consent of all three parties, and the 1922 boundary kept. Churchill was party to the 1925 agreement, but under much changed circumstances: not as a Liberal minister in Lloyd George's coalition government but as a Conservative minister in a Conservative government.

By 1921 Lloyd George and Churchill were moving apart. Winston had not wanted the Colonial Office, but rather his father's old office as Chancellor of the Exchequer. He and the Prime Minister clashed on foreign affairs, starting with Churchill's unsuccessful policy against the Bolsheviks.

Churchill was Colonial Secretary less than two years, just long enough to discover the growing dimensions of Britain's post-war imperial problems but not long enough to put his stamp upon policy. In any case there was little room for maneuver. Britain emerged from World War I pledged to support Zionist ambitions for a Jewish national homeland in Palestine and Arab nationalism in adjoining regions. The two nationalisms threatened to overlap in the British mandate of Palestine. Zionist and Arab alike soon felt betrayed by the mandate power. The French, with their own ambitions in the Middle East, also believed that Britain had tried to maneuver them out. Egyptians increasingly wanted independence from British control. And in India, the center of Empire, there emerged Mohandas K. Gandhi, a rare mixture of saint and political genius, who would lead the movement for Indian independence. The British government tried a policy of "dyarchy" in India, giving local authority to elected Indian bodies but retaining control over the central executive, although with an elected majority in the central legislature. A bloody incident, the Amritsar massacre of 1919, helped to convince Indian nationalists that only British departure from India would be adequate.

The bleak prospect in imperial affairs matched economic depression at home. By-elections ran steadily against the Lloyd George government. The Welsh wizard's time was running out; he needed an issue to run an election on. For if Lloyd George did not look a winner, he could lose his coalition. Many Conservatives wanted to campaign in the next election independently. In April, 1922, Lloyd George tried for an international success at the Genoa Conference to settle war debts and reparations. The Conference failed; the Americans would not even attend. Worse, Russia and Germany went off to Rapallo and made a pact of mutual friendship, just what Churchill had most feared would happen.

Against this background, the Chanak crisis blew up—or perhaps

Lloyd George blew it up. In 1920 the Treaty of Sevres had made peace with Turkey, who lost large chunks of Asia Minor and saw the Dardanelles Straits internationalized and allied garrisons established along both sides of the strategic waterway. But Turkey had a new nationalist leader, Mustafa Kemal, the Turkish hero of Gallipoli. Greek ambition had led to claims to the port of Smyrna and its hinterland; Turkish nationalists wanted the Greeks out. When Kemal routed the Greek forces, Smyrna fell amid scenes of massacre. Kemal's forces now headed for the Straits and Constantinople, soon reaching the international neutral zone along the Straits at Chanak, where there was a small British garrison. Lloyd George determined to hold his ground. He appealed to France and Italy while Churchill, just won over to Lloyd George's side, called on the Dominions for aid. France and Italy were cold; only New Zealand and Newfoundland showed any support for Britain. The Canadian government and British Labour both viewed Lloyd George's policy as reckless. Skillful dealings with the Turks by General Harington on the scene prevented war. On October 11, 1922 a pact securing the neutral zone, pending a new peace treaty, was signed. The Chanak crisis was over. In the end Kemal got Constantinople while the Straits remained demilitarized.

From the beginning, Churchill had argued that Lloyd George was backing unreasonable Greek claims and that Kemal represented a nation and a viable national policy with which Britain should come to terms. He reminded the Prime Minister of the dangers of arousing Mohammedan hostility to Britain throughout the Empire. The traditionally pro-Turkish Conservative Party was likewise distressed with Lloyd George's behavior, the more so since their leader, Bonar Law, had left the government the previous year because of bad health. The Prime Minister was pursuing an anti-Turkish policy against the majority of his own Cabinet, including of course Churchill, a majority of the House of Commons, overwhelming public opinion—war-weary and tired of adventures—and against his erstwhile allies, France and Italy. Lloyd George had lost his grip. Kemal's plunge at Chanak brought Churchill, almost alone, over to Lloyd George's side. Churchill, wanting a stable settlement in the area, believed Britain must restrain the aggressor. This had first been Greece, Churchill believed, but not after Smyrna. Churchill's conversion only meant that he would go down with his Prime Minister.

To the Tories, the two mad-men of pre-war days were on the loose again.

On October 10, the Cabinet, led by Lloyd George, decided to fight a general election on a Coalition ticket. Lloyd George evidently believed he had national sentiment united behind his policy. He did not even have a united coalition. The Tory M.P.'s, meeting on October 19 at the Carlton Club, heard Stanley Baldwin denounce the Prime Minister. Bonar Law had indicated already that he would return to lead the Tories if they left the coalition. This they now voted to do. The same afternoon Lloyd George resigned. He never held office again.

CHAPTER FIVE

The Tory Years: 1922 – 1929

Andrew Bonar Law became Prime Minister and soon chose his Cabinet. Stanley Baldwin, who had led the movement within the coalition against Lloyd George, became Chancellor of the Exchequer. Lord Curzon, who had left Lloyd George at the eleventh hour, retained the Foreign Office in the new government. The rest of the Cabinet, relatively unknown, were criticized as obscure second-raters when compared to the glittering talents of Lloyd George's Cabinet. Yet it had been the essence of Stanley Baldwin's charge against these glittering talents that they had become consumed by their own self-esteem, had grown negligent of the people whose servants they were, and were callous and arrogant in the exercise of power. These were certainly charges which could not then be leveled against Bonar Law, or Baldwin himself. On November 15, 1922 the choice was left to the people.

It had been a bitter campaign, not surprising after the smash-up of a coalition government. The glittering talents were savage in their invective. Lloyd George, more careful, sought to placate Conservatives while criticizing Labour. Bonar Law for his part was moderate enough. But other Conservatives, led by Lord Beaverbrook and his powerful *Daily Express,* repaid coalitionist invective with invective. Bonar Law campaigned on a program of minimum government activity at home and abroad, and a reduction in the personal role of the Prime Minister—in short, a repudiation of Lloyd George and all his works. That seemed to be what people wanted.

When the polling was completed, the new Parliament had 345 Conservatives, 142 Labour, 54 Asquith Liberals, and 62 Lloyd George Liberals. Churchill was not among them. His fall was less dramatic than that of 1915, but no less serious. He had been prostrated by an emergency appendicitis operation, still a serious matter before the era of antibiotics. He arrived in Dundee, weak and pale, only two days before the balloting. Yet in full health he would likely have lost, for Dundee and Churchill had drifted far apart. The stresses of war and post-war hard times had pushed the Dundee working class toward socialism. Churchill, a man of passionate independence of spirit, dreaded socialism as an illiberal force for leveling men down to the lowest common denominator. He failed to grasp why working men might see their best hopes in exchanging a measure of individuality for greater economic security. Accordingly, he flayed the British Labour Party as if it were the Russian Communist Party, a rhetorical extravagance that surely lost him many more votes than it gained him. He went down to overwhelming defeat, losing by 10,000 votes. In the campaign he had associated himself with Lloyd George's policies without compromise, and he also fell with the public rejection of them.

Bonar Law did not go on long. When he resigned as Prime Minister in May, 1923, he was dying of cancer of the throat. He had no positive program, and had avoided embracing the policy of protection that many Conservatives believed essential to Britain's post-war economy, and that with imperial preference, Lord Beaverbrook ever lusted after. The real gain in the 1922 election had been by Labour, now the second party in the nation, which had polled nearly 30% of the votes, more than both Liberal groups combined, and was now less exclusively trades-unionist and more national in composition and outlook.

Bonar Law's brief government saw Curzon negotiate a final settlement with Kemal at the Lausanne Conference, a brilliant performance in difficult circumstances by this able, temperamental man. Stanley Baldwin went to America to negotiate a final debt settlement with the Americans and returned with terms so unpalatable to Bonar Law that the Prime Minister nearly resigned rather than accept them. Thus when Law had to go, and the choice of his successor lay between Curzon and Baldwin, the selection of the latter was a surprise to many, most of all to Curzon. Yet the choice was wise, and, although Bonar Law did not clearly commit himself, was surely his own preference. Balfour had urged Baldwin's case to the King on grounds that a Prime Minister must come from the House of Commons. This argument would surface again in 1940, when the Commons' candidate would be Churchill. Perhaps more important in 1923 was the confidence Baldwin inspired, and which Curzon did not inspire, among Tory politicians. Although Curzon was bitterly disappointed, he magnanimously proposed Baldwin's election as party leader.

Baldwin was a politician of great ability tempered by a streak of indolence. He had a deep belief in conciliation tempered by a readiness to be ruthless if forced to extremity. He feared Lloyd George as a destructive force in political life and seems often to have acted as if this were a political principle. This would work in time to Churchill's benefit. But for the moment, in late 1923, Baldwin announced that the only cure for Britain's unemployment was protection, thus seizing the nettle that had so stung Tory hands in 1906 and that Bonar Law had shrunk from grasping. An election was held on December 6, 1923, essentially on this issue, and Baldwin lost. The new Parliament had 258 Conservatives, 191 Labourites, and 159 Liberals. Yet Baldwin's loss was more apparent than real. The actual votes for Conservative candidates remained relatively steady, and the issue of protection helped clear out the confusion left from the Lloyd George coalition. Coalition Conservatives now rejoined the mother party on the issue while the two Liberal factions fused in opposition to it. The election also opened the door to office to the Labour Party, which had indeed come far since the turn of the century.

In January, 1924 James Ramsay MacDonald became the first Labour Prime Minister in British history. Because he was dependent upon Liberal votes for his parliamentary majority, MacDonald could not undertake a socialist program. Perhaps the increasingly conservative Mac-Donald was content with this, and with the opportunity to demonstrate that Labour was fit to rule. Yet he himself threw doubt on this when he chose to make a controversial political charge grounds for a vote of confidence that lost him Liberal support. He then dissolved Parliament in the autumn of 1924. A bitter election followed, during which the Foreign Office published a letter, forged we now know, purportedly from the head of the Communist International, Zinoviev, urging Communist seizure of power from bourgeois Labour. When Labour lost, the Left understandably charged that the election had been stolen from them by dirty politics. Yet their indecisive performance in office probably did Labour greater harm. The Zinoviev letter simply had the effect of making the government look foolish for having negotiated with the Soviet government which was evidently plotting its overthrow. And intelligent people, including the King, had doubted the letter's authenticity anyway. Nor did Labour lose most, actually raising its percentage of the electorate, although reduced to 151 seats. The real losers were the Liberals, down to 40 seats, while Baldwin returned in triumph with 419 seats. For his part, Baldwin had renounced protection, leaving the Liberals without a campaign issue. This also brought the return of Winston Churchill to the Conservative Party.

Churchill's defeat at Dundee in 1922 had been due in no small part to the fact that the Dundee electorate had moved Left. But Churchill seemed also moving—to the Right. The most strident notes of his 1922 campaign had been anti-socialist. He was disenchanted with Lloyd George as well, and their relations had been strained in recent years. Yet he could hardly return to a Conservative Party led by Bonar Law, who profoundly distrusted Churchill, and would never have given him office. In the 1923 general election Churchill stood for West Leicester as a Liberal Free Trader, true to his political principle of cheap bread for the people—a principle Winston had inherited from his father. It also revealed his continuing concern for the British working man. But again Labour, to which British working men increasingly turned, got Winston's hardest blows. Churchill was also haunted by taunts of the Dardanelles, and he lost again.

When the Liberals supported a Labour Government in 1924, Churchill became a political independent, and stood in a by-election in the Abbey Division of Westminster as an "Independent Anti-Socialist" candidate with considerable Conservative support. The Conservative constituency association, however, ran their own candidate, who beat Churchill by 43 votes in a poll of 20,000. During this campaign, Balfour had supported Churchill, as had Lord Beaverbrook. Baldwin was friendly, although he refused to dictate to the local constituency association to withdraw their candidate in Churchill's favor. But in fact, Churchill had by now gained his approval.

In the 1924 general election he stood as a "Constitutionalist" for Epping Division of Essex, supported by the Conservative constituency association, and won. He held the seat for twenty-one years, moving in 1945 to Woodford, which he held for his last nineteen years in Parliament. Churchill's return to favor was spectacular. Baldwin offered him the post of Chancellor of the Exchequer, which Winston's father had held and he had so wanted, even though finance was one of the subjects Churchill knew least about.

It was a dazzling return from political exile. For two years Churchill had been a man without a party, pursued by his past record. Post-war publications in both Britain and Australia had generally favored official service viewpoints, and were harshly critical of Churchill's conduct at the Admiralty. He determined to state his own case, which he did in *The World Crisis* running to several volumes appearing between 1923 and 1927. It in turn provoked new criticism. Perhaps because he wrote chiefly to defend himself, Churchill's account in *The World Crisis* is the most partisan of all his writings in argument and evidence.

With a sense of relief Churchill could turn from old controversies to new duties. As a devoted Free Trader, Churchill was Baldwin's pledge that he would abide by the electorate's decision and not resurrect protection. Baldwin also rather liked Winston, probably feeling that Churchill had been unfairly knocked about in recent years. Respectful of Churchill's great capacity for work, he could hope that Winston in the government would be safely detached from Lloyd George. Churchill, for his part, told Baldwin he had done more for him than Lloyd George ever had, and pledged unswerving loyalty. The happy prodigal was home.

In 1925 Winston dropped his "Constitutionalist" label, formally rejoining the Conservative Party and the Carlton Club, the London social home of the Tories. Those Conservatives who had stayed with Lloyd George in 1922 had all preceded Churchill in their return to the official party. One of these, Austen Chamberlain, became Foreign Secretary in Baldwin's government of reunion. His work in securing the Locarno agreements, which had cast some pale sunlight through the storm clouds of international affairs in 1925, gained him the Nobel Peace Prize, and gave early distinction to the Baldwin government.

In fact, the Ruhr occupation of 1923 by France when Germany defaulted on some reparations payments had marked a temporary low point in international affairs, followed by a season of gradual improvement. The Germans had reacted to occupation by passive resistance. A sharp inflation occurred when the German government provided wages by printing money. In November of 1923 this inflation reached its zenith of 4,200 trillion marks to the dollar, wiping out the savings and economic security of the German middle classes. This willful act of the German government, and not the abortive post-war leftist risings, constituted the real German social revolution. That same November, 1923 saw the failure of a coup in Munich led by the rising National-Socialist figure, Adolf Hitler. His turn would come later.

An intense nationalist, but traditional politician, Gustave Stresemann, led Germany into negotiations to end passive resistance, inflation, and French occupation. A change in the French government facilitated this. The reparations issue was handed to an expert commission headed by the American General Dawes. Its report, the Dawes Plan, submitted in April of 1924, led to economic stability in Germany and a more moderate rate of reparation payments. To help restore financial stability in Europe a loan was raised, largely in America. This began a process of funneling U.S. loans into Germany, where they were turned into reparation payments to the Allies, who passed them on to America as debt payments. Such was the twisted legacy of past disorder. It had to be a forecast of coming early sorrow, which would duly arrive in the Wall Street Crash of 1929 and a yet more terrible era of international economic anarchy.

But the Dawes Plan generated a more positive international climate in 1924, and led into the Locarno agreements of 1925. Stresemann suggested to France a treaty of mutual guarantee of the Rhine frontier of the two countries, guaranteed also by Britain, Italy, and Belgium. Because this meant voluntary German recognition of the Versailles delineation of Germany's western frontiers, it was understandably well received in the West and the Treaty negotiated. In September, 1926

Germany entered the League of Nations, seemingly marking her formal restoration to the community of nations. In 1928 came the Kellogg-Briand Pact, renouncing war as an instrument of national policy, which by 1933 had been accepted by 65 nations, some signing with reservations.

These happy public events obscured less happy sounds heard out of the darkness. For dark and obscure were the activities of General von Seeckt, Chief of the German Army directorate in the 1920s. The disarmament provisions of Versailles were flouted by Seeckt, with full German government knowledge. Short-term enlistments allowed the 100,000 man army to serve as a training establishment for a potentially much greater army. Russia was busy manufacturing artillery, tanks, military aircraft and poison gas for the German army. Swedish armaments flowed into Germany. In 1925 the allied Military Control Commission had bluntly reported that systematic violation of the Versailles Treaty was being practiced. The same year a new treaty of Russo-German friendship was signed.

This was most ominous for the small states of eastern Europe, especially Poland. The Locarno agreements had concerned only Germany's western frontiers. While Germany smiled to the West, it scowled upon the Slavic East. Yet so great was the desire for peace and tranquility in the West that the smiles were accepted at face value and the scowls ignored. By 1930 the last allied soldiers left the Rhineland, thus securing a major goal of Stresemann, who had died the year before, that of "driving France back from trench to trench."

In October, 1929, the same month Stresemann died, the New York Stock Exchange crashed. As American investors ran for shelter, funds ceased to flow from the new world to the old, quickly showing how artificial the European prosperity was. A deepening economic crisis in Germany was paralleled by the rising strength of the Nazi Party of Adolf Hitler, which polled 6,500,000 votes in the 1930 elections and more than doubled that figure by 1932. The pale sunlight of Locarno had radiated no life-giving energy. Now, to economic distress was added ideological menace. Hilter's henchman, Joseph Goebbels, proclaimed: "As the wolf bursts into the flock, so we come."

Churchill had originally favored a generous post-war policy toward Germany, thus enrolling her among the world's satisfied, and hence stable, nations. Gradually, he came to fear this would not be achieved.

Throughout the balmy days of the spirit of Locarno, Churchill remained cautious. He noted that the idealism of the Kellogg Pact did not itself assure peace, which would require "more unified structures" in the future. He had by 1929 already discerned "the drum-beat of new antagonisms" in Germany. Churchill warned that peace would demand "the greatest exertions . . . over a long period of years."

But in the years before 1929, Churchill's duties were not in foreign but in domestic affairs. The British people, profoundly exhausted by the strain of the preceding decade and more, were anxious for tranquility. Baldwin was anxious to provide such a policy. Churchill himself would later call it a capable, sedate government. Perhaps it would be more accurate to call it a government of capable men put in unusual offices. Churchill himself, while he worked hard, had little instinct for finance. His friend Birkenhead, a great legal mind, made an odd Indian Secretary. Austen Chamberlain, who had financial experience, was a Foreign Secretary of limited knowledge. Perhaps the man best-placed in the government was Austen's half-brother, Neville Chamberlain, who became Minister of Health, where he did good work.

In truth, Baldwin was determined to have in his government old coalitionists like Churchill and Austen Chamberlain and Birkenhead, but had a hard time placing them. Tom Jones, a faithful Cabinet secretary, had given Baldwin the good advice of appointing Winston to one of the service ministries, "the one with the most work." But Baldwin gave Churchill the Treasury, evidently because Neville Chamberlain did not want it, according to Jones' diary. In this somewhat haphazard way Churchill came to grapple with economic problems he poorly understood at a time of grave world economic insecurity.

When Churchill presented his first budget to the Commons on April 28, 1925, it provided for a return to the gold standard. Britain had firmly tied its economy to gold only in the nineteenth century, and then only after long debate. By the opening of the twentieth century, the gold standard had become almost universal among industrial nations despite the sometimes constricting effects of using so scarce a commodity as gold as the sole basis for money. This policy could at times become very acute when industrial development was increasing real wealth at a rapid rate. Yet by the 1920s the gold standard had become, however irrationally, for most Britons the natural basis of international finance, and London its natural headquarters. The war had disrupted this arrangement, but in 1918 an expert committee had recommended an early return to the gold standard at the 1914 rate of one pound sterling equalling $4.86 (U.S.).

The only trouble with this was that the world of 1918 was not the world of 1914. The overwhelming economic power of the United States was the new truth of the world economy. Britain, in particular, had lost traditional overseas markets. Her staple industries, once the backbone of her export trade, were often now out-dated, ill-run, and faced vigorous new foreign competition. Unemployment figures in these staple industries told their own story. In 1925 one third of the shipbuilding work force was unemployed, over fourteen per cent in woolen manufacture, and over eight per cent in cotton. A quarter of the iron and steel workers were unemployed, as were a fifth of the workers in shipping. But the touchstone was coal-mining, not because distress here was greatest, but rather because here labor relations were most exacerbated. If there was to be serious industrial conflict in Britain, it would come in the coal fields. The Ruhr occupation had disrupted the continental coal supply, giving British coal an artificially good year in 1924. Unemployment in the coal fields dropped under six per cent, but in 1925 it went back over fifteen per cent.

To return to gold at pre-war parity with the dollar meant deflation and higher prices for British goods abroad, for the floating rate of parity late in 1924 was about $4.40 to the pound. John Maynard Keynes, the most brilliant economist of the age, argued against the return. Yet official Treasury opinion, several expert committees, including one appointed by the 1924 Labour government, and most public sentiment favored the return to gold. It promised cheaper food prices for the worker, always a strong argument with Churchill. His 1925 budget also embodied more generous pensions for them and reduced direct taxation which he hoped would stimulate consumption. Churchill's first budget was well received. For Baldwin, it was a proof that the good old days he so ardently desired had indeed returned. The London financial community was generally pleased. The Labour Party opposed the return only on the grounds that the time was not yet right, and did not even criticize the rate of dollar parity. But the critical impact of deflation and the return to gold fell on the mining industry. Exported coal would cost more in world markets now unless its production costs could be cut. But the chief cost of coal production was the miners' wages. Thus crisis was precipitated in that very industry where the worst labor-management relations existed. Later Lord Birkenhead observed he would have thought the miners' leadership the most stupid men he knew, if he had not also met the owners.

Accordingly, when wage cuts were proposed by the owners, the miners called upon their cautious allies, the transport and railway workers, to threaten a general embargo on coal transport. The Baldwin government, committed to conciliation by the conviction of the Prime Minister, and caught unprepared, gave way to this threat on July 31, 1925, known to the Left as "Red Friday" in contradistinction to the unhappy Friday in 1921 when the triple alliance of unions had cracked. A Royal Commission under Sir Herbert Samuel was appointed to survey the coal industry's problems. In the meantime the government provided a subsidy for nine months to keep miners' wages unchanged. The government also set about an emergency scheme for keeping essential services functioning if threatened with something like a general strike again. It soon would be.

In March of 1926 the Samuel Commission gave in its report, which recommended many long-term improvements in efficiency, equity and working conditions for the coal industry. It was the short-term proposals that caused trouble: the commission rejected nationalizing the industry or any continuation of the government subsidy and accepted the owners' argument that in the immediate crisis there would have to be lower wages or longer hours. The miners' position was blunt and brief: not a penny off the pay, not a minute on the day. The miners' leadership rather expected the Trades Union Congress, the British trades union leadership, to stand with them in the last ditch, if necessary by recourse to "direct action," that is, a general strike. A general strike, of course, raised directly the issue of the public interest, that is, whether the entire nation should suffer because of an industrial conflict in one industry. And the public interest was the responsibility of the government. The T.U.C. leaders were not enthusiastic to precipitate such a potential confrontation of the unions against the government, which could probably command wide public support. "Direct action" was also a concept that undermined the very reason of existence for the Parliamentary Labour Party. So the miners had very luke-warm allies, while the T.U.C. leadership worked hard for conciliation, as did Baldwin and Birkenhead for the government.

Late on the night of May 2 the negotiations collapsed, ostensibly because "direct action" had begun when printers at the *Daily Mail* refused to set up an anti-labor editorial. In fact the negotiations failed more for lack of a formula and through the sheer physical exhaustion of the negotiators, chiefly Baldwin.

The General Strike of 1926 from May 3 to May 12 was of no help to the miners. It blasted the myth of the efficacy of "direct action" within a democratic society, something which seems to have to be demonstrated about once every generation. The government was prepared in 1926—for example, road transport was able to take up much of the slack from reduced rail transport. The unions achieved impressive solidarity in going out, but their action did not enlist broad public sympathy. Neither government nor T.U.C. wished to abandon moderation. While there were violent incidents, there were also episodes of good will. No life was lost.

When the dockers showed signs of taking a tougher position toward government movement of foodstuffs, both the T.U.C. leadership and Baldwin were anxious to find a way out. On the evening of May 8 Baldwin used the radio to appeal for an end to the strike in dramatic terms: "Can you not trust me to ensure a square deal for the parties—to secure justice between man and man?" The T.U.C. leadership accepted—indeed it was all Baldwin would promise them—and called off the strike. Baldwin firmly checked any employer ideas about penalizing strikers. The miners, however, stayed out, their problem unresolved. When they went back it was largely on the owners' terms.

The events of the General Strike of 1926 were disastrous to Churchill's reputation with the British Left. To Churchill the General Strike attacked the very basis of parliamentary democracy through the "direct action" approach. He believed the real issue was a constiutional one and that it must be met firmly. While this might well have become the ultimate issue, if no way was found out of the early-May impasse, it was certainly not the T.U.C.'s intent to challenge the constitution. They therefore deeply resented Churchill's violent reaction. Indeed, Baldwin was sufficiently concerned by Winston's vehement feelings that he gave Churchill the task of publishing a government newspaper, *The British Gazette*, in hope of keeping him thus occupied while the Prime Minister sought conciliation. Churchill's behavior as editor of *The British Gazette* has been called one of the less attractive episodes in his career. It led Lord Beaverbrook, hardly a man of the Left, to conclude that Winston had in him the stuff of which tyrants are made. The paper itself, inflammatory in tone, made no pretense at objectivity. It compared very badly to the performance of the British Broadcasting Corporation, state-supported but much more fair-minded in its news reporting.

Indeed, Churchill was so worked up he was prepared to advocate escorting food convoys through London by troops with bayonets fixed and guns loaded. Sir John Anderson, the civil servant of great ability responsible for these operations, sharply but fairly told Winston to stop talking nonsense. Fortunately for Churchill's reputation, the *Gazette* lasted only eight issues, and Winston had been successfully restrained from all sort of possible follies. How to explain such reckless behavior in a middle-aged and experienced politician who should have known better? These were, after all, British citizens against whom Churchill proposed the soldiers fix bayonets and load their rifles. Churchill put his case to Baldwin on May 4 when he said there were two disputes on: the General Strike, which was a challenge to constitutional government and upon which the government must not compromise. And there was the dispute in the coal industry in which the government should "take utmost pains to reach a settlement in the most conciliatory spirit."

Churchill was faithful to this statement in his conduct during and after the General Strike. As soon as the strike was called off, Churchill joined the forces of conciliation in the Cabinet. When an exhausted Baldwin departed for a vacation on the continent in the autumn, Churchill took up much of the government burden of trying to assist negotiations in the coal industry. For several months Churchill labored at these negotiations, playing a leading role during the autumn when Baldwin was absent. Indeed, Tom Jones wrote Baldwin in September that now Winston was all but bullying the owners to give generous terms to the miners. The Prime Minister wrote to Churchill reminding him of the limits of what his government could accept responsibility for doing. In mid-September, Baldwin returned to take over from Churchill, but had no more success in getting a generous settlement. Baldwin was unwilling to see the government get into such responsibilities as compulsory arbitration, believing every further step into the dispute the government took heightened agitation for nationalization of the industry. The owners held the economic advantage, and Baldwin would not go much beyond offering good offices. So the miners went back in the winter to longer hours, lower pay, and no national standard contract. Churchill's eight-days' madness in May earned him denunciation from every quarter: Baldwin's Conservative Party advisers, responsible civil servants, and the entire British Left. Winston's work at conciliation of nearly six months' duration was hardly noticed.

Indeed, no one seemed to wish to be reminded of the General Strike. Organized labor put it aside as something not to get into again. In 1927 legislation formally declared as illegal strikes intended to coerce the government. The political levy on trade unionists (who were the financial backbone of the Labour Party) was restricted to members who elected to pay it, whereas previously an unwilling member had to contract out. That is, trade unionists need not contribute to their unions' political funds unless they gave written notice of their willingness to do so (contracted in), reversing the terms of the Trades Unions Act of 1913 which provided for the automatic deduction of the political levy unless the unionist gave written notice otherwise (contracted out). Human nature being what it is, the 1927 legislation had the practical effect of reducing the political funds available to Labour. Thus British Trade Unionism and the Labour Party alike felt, with some reason, that Baldwin had fallen short of his talk about a square deal. Yet the same bitterness did not attach to the Prime Minister as surrounded the more ostentatious Churchill. (Note, however, that when Labour secured a clear majority in 1945, the act of 1927 was by an act of 1947 repealed.) Churchill had wished to couple the requirement of contracting in, which he approved, to a compensating measure of an Exchequer grant of £300 to defray election expenses of every candidate polling a set minimum vote, thus easing the campaigns of poor men. This figure would meet most expenses of a Labour candidate. The concept is typical of Winston's twin attitudes of hostility to what he believed was an enforced trade union and socialist solidarity, and his desire to provide equity and opportunity for the working class.

As Chancellor of the Exchequer, Churchill continued a policy of dependence upon traditional financial orthodoxy. He proposed to encourage industry and agriculture by derating, that is, off-setting local taxation by subsidies from the national exchequer. Neville Chamberlain, who was laboring on poor law and local government reform and was thus intimately concerned with local rates, opposed the extent of Churchill's subsidies. The two ministers clashed sharply, but finally compromised. The 1928 budget reduced the local rates burden on industry and railways by 75%, and completely on agricultural land and houses; it also underwrote Chamberlain's local government reforms. As an effort to make British industry more competitive abroad, this scheme was more ingenious than successful. And as a sop to Conservatives who wanted protection it was not successful either. As Chancellor, Churchill remained wedded to monetary and fiscal management of the economy, an ancient British Exchequer practice running from Pitt the Younger through Peel and Gladstone down to World War II, despite some imaginative exceptions. By the end of World War I, Britain's whole economy, and place in the world economy, required more than fiscal management.

At the core of Britain's history in the twentieth century is the relationship between her long political inheritance as a great world power, possessing a vast empire, and concerned with affairs everywhere, and the reality of her strength to play such a role. In the 1920s, narrowly conceived, this policy centered on the defense budget. Churchill as Chancellor hoped to cut service costs but he quickly clashed with the Admiralty, which argued that Britain's world-wide commerce required keeping a large number of cruisers. This class of ship had been excluded from the Washington Naval Conference agreements of 1921-22, which had fixed relative tonnage ratios for the capital ships of America, Britain, Japan, France and Italy, as well as providing a ten-year holiday on new capital-ship construction and a total tonnage limit on aircraft carriers. The Admiralty had secured five new cruisers from the Labour government of 1924 and wanted five more from Churchill in 1925, plus more in subsequent years. Churchill thought this excessive and clashed with his old friend Admiral Beatty, now the First Sea Lord. Beatty believed that Winston had gone "economy-mad," but some of Baldwin's Conservative advisers believed that Churchill was playing a deeper game, aimed at seizing control of the party from Baldwin. Whatever the case, Churchill lost the so-called "cruiser crisis" and the Admiralty got most of what it wanted—four cruisers in 1925 and three more the next year.

Churchill's position in this dispute, and his role in the development of the 10-year rule, have been combined by his critics to indict him as a prime culprit for Britain's military weakness as war approached in the late 1930s. The 10-year rule was born in 1919 when Lloyd George told the service chiefs they need not anticipate a major war within that time span. This same answer was given to the service chiefs throughout the mid-1920s. In 1928, at Churchill's urging, the government defined that the 10 years began anew every morning until the government directed otherwise. In 1932 this instruction was revoked. Critics have attributed to it much of Britain's weakness in 1939 and blamed Churchill for the slowness in the rearmament he came to demand in the 1930s. Churchill's critics have a weak case; the Royal Navy was limited not so much by the 10-year rule as by a series of international agreements running from the Washington Conference of 1921-22 through the London Naval Conference of 1930. And when Churchill did challenge the Admiralty building program he lost. The Royal Air Force that faced Hitler's Luftwaffe in the Battle of Britain was chiefly the product of technical developments of the 1930s and probably better for it. The Army suffered most by the 10-year rule. But its own internal resistance to the development of mobile, armored warfare was so strong that it is hard to feel that the politicians did it more damage than the generals.

Further, Churchill's policy was based upon a reasonable reading of the risks of war. When the risks increased, Churchill waived his opinions. For instance, he told the Commons on March 8, 1934, well ahead of his critics, that the conditions governing the defense clauses of his five budgets had changed, and therefore future British defense policy must change, too. What Britain's imperial defense most lacked in the 1920s was an effective co-ordination of political leadership and the three services, as the fate of Singapore demonstrated. This was to be Britain's chief naval base east of Malta, but work went forward erratically, was stopped by Labour in 1924, renewed in 1925, stopped again by Labour in 1929 and not renewed again until 1933. Nor did naval and air officers co-oridinate planning for its defense. All these cumulating deficiencies would be laid bare later. Yet no one foresaw an early war during the five years of the Baldwin government; when it left office World War II was still 10 years off.

The Baldwin government went to the electorate in 1929 following enfranchisement of women 21 to 30 in 1928, women over 30 having received the vote in 1918. Baldwin asked to be kept on to finish the job. The Cabinet expected victory, but got defeat. Most voters felt the Baldwin government had not done much of a job in its five years. When Labour returned 288 members to the Conservatives' 260 and the Liberals' 59, Ramsay MacDonald returned as Prime Minister. Churchill was elected at Epping, but was again out of office. He was a lonely politician in 1929, still distrusted by the men around Baldwin, and tarred with his performance during the General Strike in the eyes of Labour. He had quarreled with Beaverbrook then, and would lose Birkenhead to premature death in 1930. He had no body of support in Parliament or in the nation. Yet time was working in his favor; judgments upon his conduct during World War I were being revised, a process that would continue into the 1930s. In 1931 the penetrating observer, Harold Nicolson, wrote that "Winston Churchill is the most interesting man in England" and called him a phenomenon, an enigma: "How can a man so versatile and so brilliant avoid being considered volatile and unsound?" Thus at the opening of the 1920s Nicolson asked the essential question that would receive adequate answer only at the very end of that terrible decade of human misfortune.

CHAPTER SIX

The Locust Years: 1929–1939

Ramsay MacDonald had hardly formed his second Labour Government when he was confronted by a world economic crisis triggered by the New York Stock Exchange crash. As everyone rushed for shelter, each nation acted to protect itself. In this panic Britain was the most vulnerable because she depended most upon international trade,—i.e., upon her manufactured exports and external earnings to off-set her necessary imports, particularly of foodstuffs. By the end of 1930 both MacDonald and his Chancellor of the Exchequer, Philip Snowden, were convinced that the economic crisis required unusual steps. By that time there were 2,660,000 men drawing unemployment relief. While some people urged the remedies prescribed by J. M. Keynes of state-sponsored schemes of economic expansion, Snowden remained faithful to the old orthodoxy of government economy, cost-cutting, and lower wages in order to restore the export trades. Demands upon the Bank of England for gold redemption by frightened holders of the pound required the government to seek help abroad, mainly from New York. The foreign bankers insisted upon a balanced budget to encourage confidence in the pound. The Labour Cabinet would not agree to all the terms, because they believed the required economies would fall with punitive force upon the laboring classes. MacDonald and Snowden then, with royal encouragement, turned to the Conservative and Liberal parties for support. On August 24, 1931 a National Government led by MacDonald was announced. Since only a handful of Labour members, now called National Labour, would follow MacDonald, and with the small Liberal Party split over entering the government, its real support was Conservative. The Paris and New York bankers delivered the loans when Snowden presented, in September, a balanced budget based on raised taxation and reduced expenditures; this he achieved by cutting government employees' salaries and by reductions in unemployment benefits. On these terms the National Government secured a vote of confidence, 309 to 249.

But in mid-September a new panic set in, fueled partly by shortages in continental banks which then drew on British deposits, and partly by some agitation over pay cuts among sailors at Invergordon; this latter incident was dramatized into a mutiny. A panic run on the Bank of England led to Great Britain going off the gold standard on September 21, 1931. The standard had lasted barely six years. The government believed that to restore confidence required an election, a "doctor's mandate" for the government to do whatever was necessary to revive the economy. When the three parties in the National Government could not agree on specific remedies, each issued its own program before the election on October 27.

Although the election was generally quiet, there was much bitterness between the Labour Party faithful and those who followed MacDonald into the National Government. His own flamboyant reminders of the catastrophic inflation that had swept Germany in the early 1920s did nothing to soothe exacerbated nerves or assuage popular fears. Neither can it be said that the unemployed got much comfort or cheer from Churchill. About this time he wrote that "the vast majority must look only to re-absorption in the normal or natural industries," and he condemned public works as a method to reduce unemployment. British workers sensed little compassion in such recommendations. The National Government gained an overwhelming mandate of 60% of all votes, and returned 554 members of whom 473 were Conservative. The Labour Party, with 52 members, constituted the chief opposition. This sweeping result impressed everyone, including the British voters themselves.

Confidence appeared regained, but economic prosperity proved harder to recover. Unemployment reached a record high of over 2,800,000 in the third quarter of 1932, after which it slowly improved. Yet in 1937 unemployment was still higher than it had been in 1929. The National Government, chiefly Conservative although Ramsay MacDonald remained Prime Minister, had secured its doctor's mandate, but, like governments everywhere in the western world, it found the task of curing the nation's economic ills a long and unrewarding chore. It would be hard to say the National Government did much more than let bad times run their course.

Churchill was not among the Conservative members of the National Government. Baldwin occupied the office of Lord President and possessed in reality the chief power, and the Conservative Neville Chamberlain replaced Snowden, who became Lord Privy Seal, at the Treasury. In January, 1931, Churchill had left the "shadow Cabinet," the parliamentary leadership of his party, because of differences centered upon the future of India. Governing India had become an increasing problem as the forces of nationalism grew there. This was not a single sprout, for both Hindu majority and Moslem minority tended to grow apart. The Moslems had been granted separate electorates early in the century as Britain gradually extended political rights, leading to Hindu charges that the British were pursuing a policy of "divide and rule." The India Act of 1919 had accepted the idea that India should evolve toward dominion government at some distant date. This idea Churchill opposed, for he believed that problems of religion, caste, princely rights and differing traditions in the Indian sub-continent made self-government impossible.

In the 1920s the man who would contribute most to undoing Churchill's views had emerged as leader of the National Congress, chiefly a Hindu party. Mohandas K. Gandhi, known as the Mahatma (great soul), a man of undoubted spiritual exaltation, was at once both Hindu reformer and India's first true mass political leader. Gandhi advocated the methods of non-violent resistance, which he hoped would place an intolerable burden upon British moral principles, and push the British in the only direction a civilized nation could go—toward Indian self-government. When in 1930 the British government refused to give a definite promise of self-rule, Gandhi led a new campaign of civil disobedience. The Viceroy, Lord Irwin (later Lord Halifax), persuaded Gandhi to forego resistance, and to join discussions concerning India's future. Tragically, these round-table conferences would reveal a deep Hindu-Moslem split. When the National Government took office in late 1931, it asked approval of this policy of negotiation with Indian nationalists. Churchill feared this meant dominion self-government and laid down an amendment that the British government should not commit itself to the granting of a dominion constitution to India. Churchill's motion gained only about 40 votes. It was not Churchill but the problem of the various minorities in India that was retarding the movement toward Indian self-government in the early 1930s.

Churchill's position on India was, however, impossible. He believed that to leave the Indian subcontinent to self-government was "criminally mischievous" in the disorders and cruel fate of minorities that he predicted would follow. Baldwin saw the immediate disorders that would follow British resistance to Indian progress as a greater danger than future disorders when self-government was achieved. Churchill's position was fatally weak when challenged to produce a solution to prevent Indian unrest. In debate, Churchill spoke of British decisions and "Indian loyalty and goodwill." But as was scathingly pointed out in debate, Churchill's Indian policy did not command Indian loyalty and goodwill. Why did he then pursue such an unrealistic policy? It was partly his romanticism that led Winston to portray an India which no longer existed, perhaps never existed. But partly Churchill dreaded the future of Britain without her Empire. Such a Britain could not long command a position among the great powers of the world and Churchill shrank back from such a future specter.

As an instrument for challenging Baldwin's political position, Churchill's Indian policy also failed utterly. In an emotion-charged scene in the Commons in March, 1931, Baldwin dared his critics to depose him as party leader. The parliamentary Conservative Party supported Baldwin's Indian position. In the same month Baldwin destroyed an attempt of the press lords, Rothermere and Beaverbrook, to impose their Empire Free Trade policy on him when their candidate was defeated by the regular Conservative Party candidate, the attractive Duff Cooper, in a by-election. Churchill had blundered badly, evidently by inadvertence, when he addressed a large rally opposing Baldwin's Indian policy on the eve of the by-election. This made Churchill appear part of an extra-parliamentary plot to overthrow Baldwin and left Winston vulnerable to criticism. Esteem for Churchill within the parliamentary Conservative Party hit a new low, and not surprisingly he was not included in the National Government formed in August of 1931.

Churchill continued his drumfire of criticism against the government's Indian policy up through the passage of the India Act of 1935, which was carried in the Commons on the critical second reading 404 to 133. Throughout Churchill had led a minority of the most reactionary members of the House, and branded himself as a romantic sabre-rattler, with serious consequences when he turned to warn of real dangers in Europe. Churchill's standing in the Commons had been further damaged in 1934 when he initiated an obscure Breach of Privilege dispute against government members upon the flimsiest of evidence; he was accused of resorting to any means to seek political advantage. Perhaps the affair's worst effect was to make Winston look so reckless that no member could respect his judgment or take seriously charges he made. This would cast its shadow over his long warnings about Hitler. By 1935 Churchill's isolation in the Commons was all but complete.

This lonely, wayward giant had reached the nadir, partly self-fashioned, of his fortunes. In these years he was laboring at his magisterial account of his great ancestor, John Churchill, Duke of Marlborough, who had led a European coalition in the field against the ambition of Louis XIV of France. A dramatic theme well-suited to Churchill's temperament, it seemed to cry out for comparison with the ominous movement of events upon the European continent in the 1930s.

Churchill had acquired an old manor, Chartwell, in Kent, where he did much of his writing. Visitors there found Winston hospitable and as happy as he could be when out of office, surrounded by his family whom he deeply loved. He seemed at times to live amid a haze of smoke and flow of alcoholic beverages. Lord Beaverbrook, a careful observer, said this was not at all the case; Winston cheerfully exaggerated these aspects of his character. Cigars, for example, were frequently lit, only to be put aside and let die for the more attractive pleasures of conversation. Churchill's consumption of matches outstripped his consumption of cigars. His conversation—it was usually a brilliant monologue—dazzled the visitor just as Winston's inexhaustable energy would overwhelm him. Ponds were built, gardens moved about, laborers marshalled like troops, all to the endless flow of Winston's rich rhetoric. But Churchill at Chartwell was like a battleship mired in a mud-puddle and, as the 1930s wore on, the years out of power lengthened, and Hitler's Germany became stronger, Churchill's good humor gave way steadily to gloom.

Ramsay MacDonald, his powers failing, gave up the premiership in 1935 and Baldwin became Prime Minister again. The 1935 elections saw Labour secure 154 seats, but Baldwin's National majority of 432, of whom 387 were Conservative, was comfortably large. The new Labour leader, Clement Attlee, had seen combat in World War I. There were able young Tories too, like Anthony Eden, Harold Macmillan, and Duff Cooper. To them Churchill was someone apart, a man who had managed departments of state when they were still youngsters. He was an old and battered monument of state, who seemed to endure like granite, and perhaps he was serviceable yet.

An important part of the 1935 campaign had revolved around the universal desire in Britain for a long, secure peace, and how this could best be assured. There was a widespread desire to avoid European commitments, now held partly to blame for World War I. Churchill had shared this view, and as late as 1930 had described Britain as interested in and associated with continental affairs, but not absorbed in them. The long depression commanded domestic interest; foreign affairs seemed of remote interest. The parliamentary Labour leader from 1931 to 1935 had been George Lansbury, almost a pacifist. Ramsay MacDonald, while Prime Minister, had placed high hopes in the Geneva Disarmament Conference, which had opened in 1932.

Yet there was always a parallel theme: that in a dangerous world it was unwise to be unarmed. Churchill, speaking on the Prime Minister's hopes for progress at Geneva, warned that in the world as constituted, disarmament conferences did more harm than good. In March of 1932 the government had evidently agreed to the extent of canceling the 10-year rule, but immediately afterwards, Neville Chamberlain, the

Chancellor of the Exchequer, introduced the lowest service estimates between the wars. Confusion was general; Harold Nicolson found people wanted both "collective security" and "no political entanglement in Europe." A by-election at East Fulham, a normally Labour constituency in metropolitan London, was fought in 1933 apparently on the issue of "peace." A government majority of 14,000 in 1931 became a Labour victory of 5,000. Politicians were stunned by the result, coming only 12 days after Hitler had pulled Germany out of the Geneva disarmament talks. It was unwisely assumed that the people wanted peace at any price. The normal Labour character of the constituency, and deep resentment there toward the government's relief policy, the "means test," was overlooked. Baldwin, in particular, came to believe it would be hard to get the electorate to accept rearmament. While it was true that the successful Labour candidate belonged to the extreme pacifist wing of the party, it was the poor housing and prolonged unemployment that probably led most electors in East Fulham to turn out the government candidate.

Similarly subject to misinterpretation was the "Peace Ballot" begun by the British League of Nations Union in October 1934 with the final tabulation of about 11,500,000 replies announced in June 1935. Over ten million respondents favored proposals for an all-round reduction in armaments, the abolition of the private manufacture of arms, and finally the abolition of national armaments by all nations. More difficult to interpret was the response to the proposal that an aggressor should be stopped by resort to force if necessary. About six and three-quarters million accepted this, while over two million opposed it, and another two million gave no opinion. At the time most stress was placed on how much less public support this proposal commanded than the others; the clear majority ready to resort to arms if necessary was not so much noted.

Yet there was some significant movement at the grass-roots level. By 1935 the Labour Party, led by Hugh Dalton on the National Executive, and Ernest Bevin among the Trade Union leadership, was moving to the position that Hitler would have to be resisted, even by force. But the wounds of 1931 cut deep. As late as 1937 Attlee would write that there could be no agreement over foreign policy between a Labour opposition and a capitalist government. The government, for its part, continued to try to do business with Hitler even after he had taken Germany out of disarmament discussions and the League of Nations in 1933. A bloody purge of the Nazi left wing in 1934 was viewed as a move toward stability in Germany. The Saar was returned by plebiscite to Germany in 1935 and the same year a British-German naval agreement was signed, which ignored some of the Versailles disarmament provisions. Neither government nor opposition were consistent in these years, both fearing Hitler, and hoping he could be restrained. But they could not agree on a foreign policy, and were divided by the bitterness of the 1931 domestic smash-up.

By 1935 Churchill was becoming the leading spokesman warning of Hitler and the need to guard against him. In late 1933 he had warned of the vigor and scope of German rearmament. Early in 1934 he began to center his attention upon air power and Britain's lack of an adequate air force and air defenses. At first Churchill's criticism of government policy did not make him friends among the opposition. In 1933 a Labour leader had warned that Churchill in office would introduce Fascist measures. Stafford Cripps denounced the government's 1935 defense program as forced upon them by "wild men like Mr. Churchill." Some young people thought him "preposterous" and perverse when Churchill warned of the catastrophe of a new war.

It was the government that first responded to Churchill's warnings. These warnings called for parity in the air and for creation of a Ministry of Defense. He predicted terrible destruction and death from the bombing of London, quite exaggerated predictions, events would prove, as were some of his estimates of German air strength. But on the central point, Churchill was quite right; the Royal Air Force had sunk to sixth in the world by the early 1930s and its entire aircraft equipment was antique. The government did respond to Churchill's warnings, and by 1939, just in time, the R.A.F. possessed first-class fighters and the world's best air defense system, incorporating radar detection and radio-directed interception.

Both Churchill and the government were less sensitive to the threat of the German army. Churchill tended to believe that static warfare would prevail on land, and was out of touch with technical developments in mobilized, armored warfare. Indeed, Churchill even predicted at one point that the tank was obsolete as a weapon. And as late as 1939 he held the view that a single well-armed vessel could hold its own against aircraft. The test of war would falsify these predictions. He also over-estimated the damage incendiary bombs could do, although Londoners would find these unpleasant enough in 1940. Certainly Churchill's warnings were dramatic; he spoke of "the crash of bombs exploding in London and cataracts of masonry and fire and smoke. . . ." He called London "the greatest target in the world, a kind of tremendous, fat, valuable cow tied up to attract beasts of prey."[1] In Britain generally, concern about German air power overshadowed concern about the striking power of the German army. The government, for its part, left the British army in last place in its inadequate rearmament budgets, budgets regularly attacked by Labour as excessive and unnecessary.

No British politician in the 1930s saw the future with perfect clarity, but many intelligent and well informed men became convinced that Churchill was most nearly right in his warnings that German rearmament was the chief danger to world stability and peace. Some of these men held official positions and supplied Churchill with information from official sources. In June, 1935 the government invited Churchill to sit on the Air Defense Research Committee, designed to give direction to British air rearmament. Churchill accepted, while retaining a free hand to criticize the government generally. In addition, he secured the appointment of his scientific adviser, Frederick Lindemann, an Oxford professor, to the scientific committee which advised the political committee. This appointment had unfortunate results when Lindemann quarreled with his scientific colleagues. The sub-committee had to be reconstituted without Lindemann, and Churchill's own effectiveness was limited by his partisanship in the scientists' dispute. Churchill remained unhappy with the slow rate of progress; the government was distressed in turn that Churchill continued to pillory them in Parliament while enjoying access to government information on the committee. It was an awkward arrangement.

In 1935, while increasingly worried about German ambitions, the British government was confronted with a concrete case of international aggression when the Italian fascist leader, Benito Mussolini, led his country into an invasion of Ethiopia. This was unpleasant for many reasons. The British government believed they could deal with Mussolini, whom they hoped to use to restrain Hitler as well as to check Communism. The League of Nations, however, voted economic sanctions against Italy. The British Foreign Secretary, Sir Samuel Hoare, had been vocal in calling for joint League action, but he most desired a settlement that would end an embarrassing affair. He and the French Prime Minister, Pierre Laval, prepared a partition plan giving Mussolini the most fertile regions of Ethiopia and the Ethiopian emperor thin compensation in Somaliland. A press leak of this proposal destroyed Hoare, who resigned when British opinion denounced the Hoare-Laval Pact as a betrayal of collective action under League sanction. But that collective action was ineffective, the British public showed no readiness for war, and by the summer of 1936 Mussolini possessed all of Ethiopia. Churchill's position was as unhappy as the government's; he feared Hitler most and did not take a strong stand against Mussolini. It was the British Left that was most outraged by Italy's action. Mussolini helped convince the Labour Party that aggressors respected only strength, not words.

Ethiopia was not fully conquered when Hitler on March 7, 1936 remilitarized the Rhineland in violation of the Versailles Treaty. Few British seemed to recognize the crucial importance of a remilitarized Rhineland in barring the door to the vital Ruhr industrial area to attack from the West, thus enabling Hitler to act more boldly on his eastern frontier. Public opinion held the view that the Germans were only "walking into their own backyard." Neither British nor French service advisers recommended action to their governments; indeed, neither army was geared to the mobile action that would be required. Even as careful an observer as Anthony Eden was not prepared to go beyond mildly critical words over the Rhineland. This event truly concerned Churchill, who correctly had his eye on the chief threat, but in debate he pulled his punches for he hoped to exchange words of criticism for the power of office. This was a politician's choice, and Churchill lost both ways: he muffled his criticism of British inaction toward Hitler's move, and he didn't get the job. The position Churchill wanted was the newly-created office of Minister for the Co-ordination of Defense. Baldwin chose Sir Thomas Inskip, a lawyer quite unfamiliar with defense matters. Baldwin by 1936 had apparently suffered sufficient grief from Churchill that he had come to accept Bonar Law's dictum that Churchill was less dangerous out of office. Winston, however, was deeply shocked that Baldwin did not choose him. As it turned out, the new post had almost no effective powers, so Churchill was fortunate to be left out, however deeply it hurt at the time.

The overriding impression of the mid-1930s is that of confusion. Individuals and parties alike were stumbling around for a foreign policy. Some began to stumble into each other. Perhaps Adolf Hitler was pushing them together. One group, called Focus, founded in 1935, included Churchill and some old political friends. Never too significant of itself, Focus was one of the forces that led into the "Arms and the Covenant" movement, which came to prominence in 1936 in a search to make collective security effective through the League of Nations. Churchill himself had come to accept collective action through the League only slowly, as he grew convinced that Britain's security required it. He summed up this view in October, 1935, when he said that Britain's fortunes "are inseparably interwoven with the fortunes of the world. We rise or we fall together." In December of 1936, the T.U.C. secretary, Walter Citrine, chaired a mass rally which Churchill addressed. Thus ten years after the General Strike Churchill was again in touch with the British Left. Ethiopia, the Rhineland, and government drift all made Churchill look better to the Left than he had in a long time. Many agreed with Churchill's verdict on Baldwin that one cannot have all the power without having also to accept the chief responsibility.

But old distrust could not blow away overnight. Churchill soon gave new cause to those who doubted that he was a suitable candidate to exercise the power and bear the responsibility. In 1935 the deeply beloved King George V had died, and his eldest son, a 41-year-old bachelor, succeeded him: Edward VIII. Edward wished to marry Mrs. Wallis Simpson, an American woman already once divorced, and in the process of divorcing her second husband. The code of British society, working class as well as upper class, was against Edward's aspiration. Divorce still carried a moral stigma, and most British desired conventional propriety in the royal family. Mrs. Simpson just did not fit into this picture. Indeed Edward's relations with her were studiously ignored by the British news media until Edward forced a crisis by making his intentions clear to the government. Baldwin in turn made clear that Mrs. Simpson was not acceptable to the public, to the present government, or any potential government. Edward, choosing the woman he loved over the crown, abdicated in December, 1936. During the brief public crisis only one prominent politician had rallied to the King: Churchill. Always insensitive to conventional sentiment, Churchill quite failed to read the public mood. He also believed Baldwin, whom

Winston had come to view as his enemy, was forcing Edward's hand. When Churchill pleaded in Parliament for delay on December 7, 1936, the House of Commons shouted him down, an unusual and terrible humiliation. Winston was utterly without support in Parliament for his position. The association of the press lords, Rothermere and Beaverbrook, with Churchill only made his motives appear suspect. As the worried young Conservative, Harold Macmillan, observed, Winston had forfeited all the gains he had made with Arms and the Covenant. Churchill, always unconventional, himself half-American, and an incurable romantic in his attitudes toward the monarchy, appears to have acted from honorable motives in the abdication crisis, but this did not save him.

The Duke of York, shy, highly-strung, and cursed with a stutter, accepted the duty abandoned by his brother and became King George VI. Courageous, and fortunate in marriage, George VI and his gifted wife, Queen Elizabeth, were crowned on May 12, 1937. Baldwin shared the public cheering almost equally with the royal pair. His zenith was Churchill's nadir. But now very tired, Stanley Baldwin resigned as soon as the coronation was accomplished. Neville Chamberlain, the strong man of the National Government as Chancellor of the Exchequer since 1931, became Prime Minister, thus achieving the office his father and half-brother had both sought and failed to attain. Chamberlain's government had no place in it for Churchill, toward whom the new Prime Minister had little sympathy. The abdication crisis had divided only Churchill from all the rest.

The Spanish Civil War threatened to divide political Britain as deeply as it divided the Spanish themselves. That civil war erupted in the summer of 1936. It was bitter and prolonged because it brought catharsis to forces of conflict long building in Spain. It was virtually a struggle of the evolving forces of industrialism and democracy against the continued existence of agrarian feudalism. Regionalism, anticlericalism, obscurantism, and the confused character of the Spanish Left, which contained both anarchists and communists, added a complexity that nearly defies description. The surface conflict was between the republican government of the Left, installed in power by popular vote early in 1936, and a group of Fascist-inclined officers led by Francisco Franco. Each side in the conflict sought help, the government from the also newly-installed French government of the Left led by the socialist Leon Blum, and from Russia. Franco appealed to Mussolini and Hitler, who responded swiftly with aircraft and in time with pilots, troops, and tanks as well as much small arms. Russian aircraft and tanks came to the republican government more slowly and in lesser amounts. In January of 1939 the chief republican center, the city of Barcelona, fell, followed by Madrid in March. Franco ruled over a ravaged land. Nearly 40,000 Italian troops had aided him, and German bombers had contributed much, including an attack upon the Basque town of Guernica which called forth Pablo Picasso's great painting of horror, suffering, desperation and outrage.

Picasso expressed the feelings of the world's Left, and young people from many nations fought in the forlorn effort to preserve the Spanish Republic. But this was not the response of the British government, which labored to set up a non-intervention committee in London representing all the great European powers. Only Britain and France observed the policy of non-intervention which Germany, Italy, and Russia reduced to a joke. As non-intervention failed as a policy, British Labour swung against it. The Spanish Civil War became the great public issue dividing the British Left from the British Right. Thus it separated Churchill from his natural allies of the Arms and the Covenant movement. He greatly valued the stability he thought the institutions of monarchy and religion provided, and correctly saw that the forces of the moderate Left in Spain were becoming increasingly hostages of the Communists as the Civil War progressed. Yet German and Italian intervention also dismayed him. Thus he tended to support the government policy of ineffective non-intervention and allowing events to run their bloody course. Not until late in 1938 did he finally come to the conclusion that Franco's victory was also Hitler's and Mussolini's victory. Again, the price was no unified position on foreign affairs reaching across the spectrum of British politics. The British government, free of effective criticism, could pursue with impunity its policy of appeasement.

That policy as originally defined was an attempt to restore order to international affairs by redressing legitimate grievances, particularly those arising from World War I. In this sense, appeasement had been practised by every British government right from Lloyd George's efforts to mitigate the harshest terms of the Versailles settlement. Two conditions had supported this policy in the 1920s: a rational, democratic government in the Weimar Republic that would seek redress of German grievances within the limits of peaceful change; and the ultimate sanction of superior force at the disposal of the Allies. Churchill's own views are on record:

> *Appeasement in itself may be good or bad according to the circumstances. Appeasement from weakness is alike futile and fatal. Appeasement from strength is magnanimous and noble, and might be the surest and perhaps the only path to world peace.*[2]

Neville Chamberlain's name is forever associated with the policy of appeasement. He took over the policy in hard times; Allied military superiority had vanished; the Nazi regime's demands were stridently advocated. Chamberlain ardently sought to negotiate differences between nations. An upright man of narrow but real ability, and of great confidence and determination, his approach to international diplomacy savored of the Birmingham businessman closing a deal. He tended to believe that business could always be done, that rational men all stood to gain from agreements personally negotiated. In such talks a man's word was his bond.

Appeasement as a policy had its local triumphs. A treaty was negotiated with the government of Eire in 1938 which settled issues outstanding since the 1922 treaty, largely on Irish terms. Among other concessions, Britain gave up the use of naval bases in Irish ports, soon to become a tragic mistake. A thoroughly exasperated Churchill attacked these provisions in a violent speech. But the grave danger of appeasement as a policy lay in the definition of legitimate grievances. Who decided what grievance was legitimate, an aggrieved Germany or an apologetic Britain? And what if German grievance conflicted with British national interest? And did the grievances of Adolf Hitler know any limit? Neville Chamberlain thought so. To an American friend, Tom Jones wrote that the Prime Minister and his associates were confident they could deal with Hitler. Jones' friend responded with a grim warning of word reaching the United States concerning the treatment of German Jews. Here indeed was the red flag of warning, the jagged psychopathic thread in the fabric of German National Socialism, which above all other signs revealed the sickness gripping the German government and people. In Hitler's Germany the violence of man against man had become the ultima ratio; the forces of death had triumphed over the forces of life.

The real failure of Neville Chamberlain and his associates was their inability, or unwillingness, to recognize evil face to face. Churchill's impetuous, romantic nature could and did lead him into a thousand blunders, but his deep and vibrant humanity saved him from the worst blunder of all. Churchill approached international affairs from the perspective of British national interest, and he had by no means rejected Hitler out of hand. But in early 1938 he firmly pronounced that "nazification" of Europe was "a danger of the first capital magnitude." As the lesser pieces disappeared from the international chess board, and Hitler's power and policy alike grew more clear, so Churchill grew in stature as the chief defender of the forces of life and chief upholder of civilization against the forces of nihilism.

Appeasement was soon in trouble. The British government was not united upon its practice. When Hoare had resigned as Foreign Secretary, the young Anthony Eden had replaced him. Eden was soon in conflict with Neville Chamberlain, who wished to take effective conduct of foreign policy into his own hands. On February 20, 1938 Eden resigned. He was replaced by the reserved but resilient aristocrat the Earl of Halifax, who was supple rather than strong. The Eden resignation was significant for several reasons: it reinforced the stubborn Chamberlain's conviction that he could always have his own way with his Cabinet—an unfortunate development in view of his general ignorance of foreign affairs. But it also revealed that some of Chamberlain's own parliamentary majority—particularly those who were closely in touch with foreign affairs—were in disagreement with their leader. Twenty-five Tory M.P.'s abstained in the vote after the debate on Eden's resignation. Some of these men tended to rally around Eden to form a new, progressive Tory group, but Eden was a cautious critic. Inevitably, those increasingly disenchanted with Chamberlain and increasingly disturbed by the rattle of arms and muffled screams of terror coming from central Europe, turned to look hopefully toward Churchill.

This polarization between Churchill and Chamberlain was largely Chamberlain's doing. Twice Churchill extended conciliatory gestures toward the Prime Minister and was twice rebuffed. Chamberlain made his reasons clear when he said that to take Churchill into the Cabinet would be to have him dominate it. Churchill continued to long for office and for the opportunity to do something, even while he continued his drumbeat of criticism of Chamberlain's foreign policy.

A heavy blow was dealt that policy when Hitler annexed Austria to

Germany on March 12, 1938, which led to Churchill calling for the construction of a Grand Alliance to stop Hitler, a theme to which Churchill would return. The fall of Austria into the Nazi grip had the effect of encircling western Czechoslovakia, which had a large, restless German minority in its Sudetenland region. Because Hitler at once began agitating for "return" of the Sudetenland to Germany, and because Czechoslovakia had an alliance with France, and because Britain could hardly sit by in a war between Hitler and the French and Czechs, a major international crisis was certain. The Soviet government declared its readiness to aid the Czechs if the French did, but the French and British governments seemed more frightened than encouraged by this. Neither western government wanted to fight Hitler over Czechoslovakia, and their entire diplomacy during the Czech crisis was directed toward escaping such a conflict.

On September 15, 1938, Chamberlain flew to Germany to negotiate with Hitler at Berchtesgaden; the most Hitler would concede was determination for the Sudetenland by plebiscite; the result would be certain to favor annexation to Germany and hopelessly disrupt the Czech strategic frontiers, then backed by well-armed Czech divisions. When Chamberlain laid this proposal before the Cabinet upon his return to London, he went further: he proposed immediate cession to Germany of all areas where more than half the population was German. This plan was jointly forced on the Czechs by the British and French, who made clear they would not fight if Czech resistance led to war.

On September 22, a hopeful Chamberlain met Hitler again, this time at Godesberg, only to be brutally informed that time was now critical; German occupation must begin in a week; on September 23, Hitler extended his deadline to October 1. A shaken Chamberlain returned to Britain and reluctantly began precautionary steps in case of war.

The military situation was reviewed with gloom in Paris and London. The French army was not prepared to move forward against Germany, the only practical way to take pressure off the Czechs. The British Chiefs of Staff had already told Chamberlain that war in 1938 would likely mean defeat for Great Britain. As time ran out, a stunned Chamberlain broadcast to the nation: "How horrible, fantastic, incredible it is that we should be digging trenches and trying on gas masks here because of a quarrel in a faraway country between people of whom we know nothing." Prague, the capital of that "faraway country", was about 625 air miles from London, or nearer than either Rome or Madrid. By comparison, it is about 800 air miles from New York to Chicago. Chamberlain continued his efforts to negotiate, pressing for another meeting, a proposal that gained Mussolini's support, who in turn pressed it on Hitler.

Reprieve came at the eleventh hour; on September 28 Hitler offered a final conference on the crisis, to meet at Munich. The parties to the Munich agreement were Hitler, Mussolini, Chamberlain, and the French Premier, Daladier; the Czechs were not invited to the conference until their fate was decided. Hitler achieved his most extreme demands. The Sudetenland would be occupied by German troops by stages between October 1 and 10 with a final line determined by an international commission, with additional plebiscite areas if necessary. The four Munich participants of September 30 would then guarantee the inviolability of the rump Czech state, once the claims of Polish and Hungarian minorities were met. Hitler also signed a paper put to him by Chamberlain that promised all future difficulties between the two powers would be resolved by consultation; the two would never go to war again.

This paper Chamberlain waved aloft as he emerged from his plane on British soil again and later from Downing Street proclaimed his belief "it is peace for our time." The nation, stunned by the suddenness with which war had threatened, in relief greeted Chamberlain as their savior. Only after this first wave of emotion was spent, did they look to see what Munich meant. A four-day debate on Munich ended on October 6 with a vote of 366-144 supporting Chamberlain. Churchill did not hold back in the debate, calling Munich a "total and unmitigated defeat" in the course of a speech of great power. He warned:

> *And do not suppose that this is the end. This is only the first sip, the first foretaste of a bitter cup which will be proffered to us year by year unless by a supreme recovery of moral health and martial vigour, we arise again and take our stand for freedom as in the olden time.*[3]

He had some supporters. Alfred Duff Cooper resigned from the Admiralty in protest. In the vote in the House of Commons, some thirty Conservatives abstained from supporting their Prime Minister; these included Churchill, Eden, Duff Cooper, and Macmillan.

Churchill's own constituency association debated a motion of no confidence in him. He defeated the motion only after a powerful fighting speech to the association.

Not until November of 1938 did Churchill, joined by Macmillan, take the extreme step of actually voting against the government. By then the fruits of Munich were more apparent. On March 15, 1939 Hitler occupied what was left of Czechoslovakia, the dictator himself traveling to Prague. Two weeks later the expansion of the British army was announced. On March 31, Chamberlain announced British and French support of Poland if Hitler's actions forced the Poles to fight. At the same time, Churchill, Eden and others laid down a motion calling for formation of a genuine National Government with emergency powers. They did not get it, yet.

The pledge to Poland made the attitude of Russia critical. As soon as Prague was occupied, Churchill urged that the Soviet Union be brought into a Grand Alliance against Hitler. But Poland herself feared Russia as much as Germany, and neither the British nor the French government was willing boldly to seek Russian association against Hitler. Hitler, for his part, was ready to offer the Soviets concrete terms while western negotiators dragged on slow conversations with the Russian government. The Russians were in the enviable position of being protected from German attack by an intervening belt of guaranteed territory. Stalin could push his price for an alliance high. In particular, he wished to safeguard the Leningrad region through Soviet control of the Baltic states. Hitler was not restrained by any ethical qualms from meeting Stalin's price. On August 23, 1939 the Molotov-Ribbentrop Pact promised Russian neutrality if Germany went to war; secret clauses partitioned Poland, which was clearly doomed by the pact. Whether the West could have prevented this by outbidding Hitler remains doubtful, for the West could offer Stalin only the risks of war without gain, while Hitler could offer solid gains without risk of war. Thus the sincerity of the Soviet negotiations with the West appears open to question at the least. On August 24 the British government reaffirmed to the House of Commons its pledge to Poland; war could only be a few days away. On September 1, 1939 Hitler invaded Poland and on September 3, Churchill returned to the post he had held at the outbreak of World War I. From the Admiralty to all His Majesty's ships at sea went out the signal: "Winston is back."

Notes to Chapter VI:

1 *Hansard,* February 7, 1934; July 30, 1934.

2 *Hansard,* December 14, 1950.

3 *Hansard,* October 5, 1938.

CHAPTER SEVEN

The Finest Hour:
1939—1941

On September 3, 1939 a somber Neville Chamberlain informed the waiting nation that the British ultimatum to Germany had expired and the two nations were again at war. Most British endorsed the view of the Trades Union Congress's resolution that war came because of the "insane ambition of Germany's rulers." The initiative belonged to Hitler; his pact with Russia isolated Poland, which was able to keep up effective resistance for barely three weeks. Germany conquered western Poland while the Soviet Union occupied eastern Poland; Russian supplies passed in generous quantity to Germany, as did munitions and iron ore from Sweden. The benevolent neutrality of Russia toward Germany was only somewhat offset by American neutrality sympathetic to Britain and France. American neutrality laws made it difficult for the democracies to tap the industrial resources of the U.S. In any case, American munitions manufacturers were as limited as the American army of less than 200,000 men in 1939. Although Mussolini had not gone to war in September, the balance of military power favored Hitler.

Chamberlain had at once taken Churchill and Eden into the government, but Labour and Liberals stayed out, while promising an electoral truce. All the dominions except Eire also went to war, although South Africa did so by a narrow margin. In India the Viceroy declared war, a step viewed by the Congress Party as a national humiliation. Further east, the Japanese government's ambitions rose as the European nations' power in Asia and the Pacific drained away.

In Britain, many steps that had come slowly in World War I went into effect at once; rationing was introduced; compulsory military service had already been started. Millions of non-essential civilians, notably school children, were moved out of London to the countryside. Naval blockade and other forms of economic warfare began at once, and a small British Expeditionary Force, at first only four divisions, crossed to France. Even this small force lacked armored support, although the war minister, Leslie Hore-Belisha, had worked hard to modernize the army. When he and the generals did not get along, Chamberlain dropped him, an uneasy hint that the difficulties of World War I might recur. A great military expansion was planned; in the meantime the military posture in the west was defensive, the French army manning the elaborate Maginot Line, a great series of defensive structures that ran from Switzerland to Belgium along the Franco-German frontier. The line was vulnerable to being out-flanked by a German thrust through Belgium and Holland; these two nations, clinging desperately to neutrality, refused to co-ordinate defensive measures with the British and French. The French politicians, fragmented and scarred by internal feuds, faced the future with gloom even while the British were at first unreasonably optimistic about the future prospect.

After Poland disappeared from the map, a lull fell over the war, encouraging the British government to feel that time was on its side. As war production ended the long depression unemployment, and the predicted bombings of British cities did not develop, there was some public euphoria, too. Even at sea there was little activity; convoying was instituted at first only along Britain's east coast. Churchill and some of his naval advisers alike tended to underestimate the submarine danger. This was partly Hitler's fault; he poorly understood sea power and Germany had only a handful of U-boats operating when war came. The chief surface action was a British triumph: three small cruisers in a brave and skillful action drove the pocket battleship *Graf Spee* into Montevideo harbor, where it was scuttled.

In late 1939 Scandinavia became the cockpit of international conflict. Russia had taken control of the Baltic states of Latvia, Estonia and Lithuania, and demanded military control of parts of Finland. When the Finns refused Soviet demands, on November 30 the Red Army attacked Finland, and met fierce resistance. The Soviet action enraged British opinion, Labour as well as Conservative, and the British government sought to aid the Finns. Military wisdom argued against this decent sympathy for Finland, for to add Russia to Germany as a declared foe would be reckless in the extreme. Nor was there any easy way to get aid to Finland. Germany dominated the southern Baltic while Norway and Sweden clutched at rigid neutrality. Churchill, as much as anyone, wished to aid Finland. In doing so he also saw an opportunity to deny vital supplies of northern iron ore to Germany. Several plans were examined; the most feasible called for an expeditionary force to sail to the Norwegian port of Narvik, and to cross the Scandinavian peninsula from there, wrecking the Swedish mines while on the way to aid the Finns. This was an ambitious scheme, even if there were sufficiently developed forces and skills to carry it out—not at all certain so early in the war. Both British and French continued to examine various plans for Scandinavian operations through the winter and into the spring of 1940. Events outran allied planning. Finland made peace with Russia on March 13. That left only the Scandinavian iron ore. Sweden and Norway both indicated opposition to any allied forces on their territory. Finally it was decided to mine the Norwegian coastal waters through which the iron ore vessels passed during the winter months to Germany. This operation was to begin on April 8, 1940.

Hitler moved simultaneously, and on far greater scale. He, too, had been concerned about Norwegian waters, particularly after February 16, when British destroyers, on explicit orders from Churchill, had penetrated into Norwegian waters to stop the German ship, *Altmark,* and remove British prisoners of war from her. Hitler's spring move was spectacular; Denmark was overrun and every major Norwegian port from Oslo to Narvik seized. The Danes did not resist, but the surprised

Norwegians fought back. Churchill hoped to inflict crushing blows on the German navy. Indeed much of the strength of the German surface fleet was either sunk or damaged in the Norwegian campaign. But it was not all one way; the British aircraft carrier *Glorious,* left without adequate escort, was sunk by German warships. But more decisive, the Germans had at once seized coastal airfields and quickly proved that they could make Norwegian coastal waters intolerable for the Royal Navy. German air control sealed Norway's fate. Neither a brave resistance nor some poorly co-ordinated allied relief expeditions to the areas of Trondheim and Narvik could save the day. The Allies left central Norway in early May, and Narvik in early June. The Norwegian monarch, his government, and a million tons of Norwegian merchant shipping passed over to Britain.

The Scandinavian affair from start to finish had displayed careful planning and forceful execution on the German side and a serious lack of these qualities on the allied side. Even effective co-ordination between the British services had been lacking. It also appeared that yet again the government had underestimated Hitler's audacity and Germany's military proficiency. As late as April 4 Chamberlain had unfortunately talked about Hitler missing the bus. Angry members of Parliament demanded an accounting from the government; some M.P.'s clearly wished to call Chamberlain personally to account for his entire ministry, in peace and war; others believed that successful prosecution of the war demanded a change at the top. A political crisis was swiftly building upon the ruins of the Norwegian campaign.

The swelling demand in the House of Commons for a change in the government was both Churchill's opportunity and his danger. Several of the strongest members in the House wanted Chamberlain out of the first place and Winston in it but they were a distinct minority. Any change of leadership had to command the support of the large Conservative majority in the House, and most of these were still intensely loyal to Chamberlain. How was power to pass from Chamberlain to Churchill without disrupting that majority? Further, the capacity of the government was to be challenged in debate upon its performance in the Norwegian campaign. But no member of the government had played a larger role in that unhappy affair than Churchill. The debate could become damaging to him. All things were uncertain when the two-day debate opened on May 7 with Chamberlain defending his record.

The Labour Party leadership proceeded warily, careful not to turn the debate into a party issue, which could only have the result of maintaining Chamberlain in power. It was rather angry Conservatives who carried the attack on the first day. Admiral of the Fleet Sir Roger Keyes denounced the government, strongly indicating it did not command the confidence of the fighting services. But the most terrible speech of the day came from Leo Amery, who raked over Chamberlain's record without mercy, and concluded by quoting to the Prime Minister the words of Oliver Cromwell to the Rump Parliament in 1653, calling upon him to resign: "In the name of God, go!"

The first day's debate, revealing the seriousness of the Tory revolt and the quality of those in revolt, led the Labour leadership to announce at the opening of the second day that they would call for a division of the House at the end of the debate, technically on a motion to adjourn, but in fact a vote of censure upon Chamberlain. He responded by appealing to his friends, and was promptly denounced for making party politics out of a national issue. It was now David Lloyd George who indicated that Chamberlain was unfit for the crisis, and he intimated that Churchill was fit. The last speech of the debate was Churchill's. Both decent instinct and political necessity made him steadfastly loyal to his leader. He defended the government with vigor. It did not matter; all the humiliations Britain had suffered under Chamberlain in peace and war were carried into the division lobbies. Chamberlain won the vote, 281 to 200. In effect it was a demand for a change, for his normal majority was not 81 but 240; some 60 of his normal supporters had abstained while about 40 voted against him.

On May 9 the political crisis moved behind closed doors. The division revealed that the government must be reformed, but no one could say to what extent it would be. Chamberlain wanted to stay on, but Tory dissidents together with Labour and Liberals now all refused his overtures to serve under him; it became clear he could not lead a remodeled government. Who could? Halifax and Churchill were the chief alternatives; on the afternoon of May 9 they met with Chamberlain and the Conservative Party chief whip. When Chamberlain asked which it was to be, Churchill sat silent. Halifax broke the silence to indicate that it would be hard to lead a war government from the House of Lords. Churchill's silence had given him the first place; the others did not dare face the House of Commons and the British public without him, so they had to take him on his own terms, as Prime Minister. At the age of sixty-five, after a long career marked by every sort of political misfortune, Winston Churchill had achieved the chief power in the state in the nation's most perilous hour. His view of that moment is on record:

> *Thus, then, on the night of the tenth of May, at the outset of this mighty battle, I acquired the chief power in the State. . . . I was conscious of a profound sense of relief. At last I had the authority to give directions over the whole scene. I felt as if I were walking with Destiny, and that my past life had been but a preparation for this hour and for this trial. . . . I was sure I should not fail.*[1]

The British politician most experienced in adversity became the statesman best suited to the nation's danger, for on May 10 Hitler launched his great offensive in the west. Chamberlain thought he could stay on in the crisis, but his hour was past; Churchill now seemed the logical choice; Labour and Liberals would serve under him. At 6 P.M. on May 10 as Hitler's armor sliced through the Low Countries, Churchill went to Buckingham Palace to receive the royal commission to form a new government. On May 13, Churchill addressed the House of Commons for the first time as Prime Minister; he offered the nation only blood, toil, tears, and sweat. He proclaimed that his policy was to wage war and his aim was to secure victory. These were bold words as the situation began to deteriorate on the continent.

Fortunately, in view of the lonely ordeal Britain was soon to face, Churchill had been able to form an all-party national coalition to fight the war. Chamberlain magnanimously agreed to serve in the government but cancer claimed his life in the autumn, when Churchill at last became leader of the Conservative Party, perhaps its most unlikely leader since Disraeli. Churchill left the domestic side of his government chiefly to the Labour politicians, at first Attlee and Greenwood. Ernest Bevin became Minister of Labour and National Service and in time entered the War Cabinet in recognition of his great strength and services, as did Herbert Morrison yet later as Home Secretary. The War Cabinet, at first five men, was reshaped and expanded several times. Only Churchill and Attlee were members throughout Churchill's coalition ministry; by 1942 Attlee was recognized as Deputy Prime Minister. Yet the War Cabinet was not the essential body in the conduct of the war, or even the defense committees that operated under it.

When Churchill became Prime Minister he also took the title Minister of Defense, indicating that he intended to manage the military side of affairs himself. In view of Winston's emotional impetuosity, and the unhappy precedent of the Dardanelles, this could have been perilous. However, Churchill's war leadership was successful for several good reasons. Churchill fitted best in the first place; his vision and energy suited the endless tasks of his job. His vigor moved the entire government to increased activity and his courage sustained weaker spirits in dark days. Further, he was fortunate in the quality of the Chiefs of Staff, with whom he worked in harness in operating Britain's military effort. General Sir Hastings Ismay became chief staff officer to Churchill, and "Pug" Ismay's great ability, common sense, and vital good humor enabled him to smooth the stresses that developed between Churchill's sweeping visions and the service chiefs' concern for the requirements to support his plans. Of these men the best were Sir Alan Brooke, Chief of the Imperial General Staff from December 1941 onwards, and Sir Charles Portal, Chief of the Air Staff after October 1940. They and their associates' great professional competence blended with Churchill's great capacity to plan and direct over the broadest vistas to give Britain an unrivaled caliber of war leadership.

All this was needed, and unflinching courage also, as the front in Flanders and France collapsed before the German onslaught in the spring of 1940. The German army had outflanked the Maginot Line, moving through Belgium and Holland, who now cried for the French and British to come to their rescue. Those forces that responded became cut off from the bulk of French forces further south as German armor broke through the French lines and reached the coast near the mouth of the Seine. The forces cut off to the north were further imperiled by the sudden surrender of the Belgian King and army on May 27. Almost the entire British Expeditionary Force, the bulk of the professional army, were caught in a narrow pocket with their backs to the sea around the tiny port of Dunkirk. From this port and nearby beaches the Royal Navy and hundreds of volunteer sailors in all sort of craft snatched the army out of the jaws of destruction. By June 4, some 338,000 men, nearly two-thirds of them British, had been carried across the Channel while the R.A.F. fought off the Luftwaffe in the skies above. Dunkirk was not a victory, but it was salvation; Britain could rearm its army, but could hardly have recreated it.

The French army could not be saved. It had been coming apart in the field even as the French government behind it had been coming apart in Paris. On June 14, Paris fell to Hitler as the French government fled and its spirit of resistance ebbed away. The frantic French government demanded that Churchill throw all possible fighter aircraft into the last-ditch struggle on the continent, and Churchill's generous spirit ached to agree, but the R.A.F. leaders insisted that the minimum force essential to home defense be retained on British airfields. The critical days in this struggle came in mid-June; Churchill yielded to his service advisers and withstood great pressures from the French. This painful decision was correct, for the French leadership was beyond rescue. Marshal Pétain, ancient hero of World War I days, came forward to secure an armistice from Hitler, which was granted on June 22. Charles de Gaulle, then a young general, escaped to Britain to lead those Frenchmen who could not accept this arrangement. He had few followers; Britain was left alone to face the triumphant Hitler, who was now joined by Mussolini, who had slithered into war just before France collapsed so as to be able to claim his share of the booty.

In a famous drawing, the great political cartoonist, David Low, depicted a British Tommy standing on the cliffs of Dover and shaking his fist toward the continent above the caption: "Very well, alone." This was certainly Churchill's conviction. He was at his best in the terrible summer of 1940 when it appeared nothing could stop Hitler. He summoned the British people to the desperate struggle to defend their island with the words: "Let us so bear ourselves that, though the British Empire and its Commonwealth last for a thousand years, men shall still say 'This was their finest hour.' " The British people responded with general national unity. Peace overtures from Hitler were brushed off. Heavy government inroads upon civil rights and traditional freedoms were accepted for the duration of the conflict. Labor could be allocated; women were conscripted; taxes drained off income, but inflation was also successfully controlled. Churchill intended to fight on, no matter what.

The defense of the British Isles made naval and air power critical. The French armistice had left the fate of the French fleet uncertain; it was presumably now non-combatant, but ultimately perhaps at Hitler's mercy. Churchill believed that he must make sure Hitler could not use the French fleet to turn the precarious balance of naval power against Britain. French ships in British ports and at Alexandria either joined de

Gaulle or were neutralized under British guard, as were French ships in the West Indies under an American guarantee. But a powerful force lay at Oran, where the British attempted negotiations to secure neutralization. When the negotiations broke down, the British fired upon the ships of their recent ally. There was bitterness in France, and among Gaullists too, but no one could doubt Churchill's determination to fight on. He announced that he and the British people were awaiting German invasion across the English Channel, and so were the fishes. His grim humor mixed with eloquent and moving flights of oratory to describe his nation's resolve. When the action at Oran was explained to the House of Commons, there was only overwhelming approval.

But more than spirit was needed. There were soon signs of German invasion preparations. As the Royal Navy still possessed a precarious superiority at sea, Germany must first drive it out of the Channel before her army could cross. Hitler counted upon his air force to accomplish this. This set the stage for the Battle of Britain. Churchill had formed only one new government department when he became Prime Minister, the Ministry of Aircraft Production. Lord Beaverbrook was charged with achieving the needed production of fighter aircraft to meet the demands of the Battle of Britain, and this, by means fair and foul, Max Beaverbrook did. The basic structure for the Air Defense of Great Britain was sound. Radar detection, supplemented by visual observation, tied into regional R.A.F. centers that could deploy by radio fighters to intercept German formations as they reached the British coast. This meant that wasteful and futile standing air patrols could be eliminated, and maximum fighter strength concentrated upon the German attackers.

Sir Hugh Dowding, Chief of Fighter Command, and his subordinate Sir Keith Park, commanding No. 11 Group, located in the critical southeast corner of England, were both strong men who held tenaciously to the exhausting task of intercepting the German formations as they arrived and refused to adopt the more spectacular tactics of massed fighter sweeps urged upon them by their professional critics. Dowding and Park were surely wise in adhering to their careful tactics, for they had to husband carefully their most precious commodity of trained fighter pilots. These men, the famous "few" to whom the nation owed so much, for their part flew to the point of exhaustion and often beyond. Fighter Command had no human margin for error and under Dowding's firm and competent command the few were sufficient. These men's valor fairly earned them Churchill's famous tribute, but in fact they only dramatized the character of modern war. They, or many times their number, would not have been sufficient if there did not stand behind them all the requisite technical services needed to refuel, rearm, repair, or even replace their aircraft. Vital also were the scientists, the "boffins" who had developed radar, and the technicians who operated it, the communications experts and skilled R.A.F. personnel who directed the sophisticated system of interception. And beyond these stood the men—and women—working long hours in the factories to provide the essential equipment, and all the other resources of a modern industrial society. In 1940 war was well on the road toward the single finger upon the button.

The Battle of Britain began officially on July 10, and raged for three months. Whereas Dowding had a clear operational plan, his opponent, the Luftwaffe commander Herman Goering, did not. He was supposed to defeat the R.A.F., batter the Royal Navy, and reduce Britain by air bombardment alone. Muddling among these aims, Goering achieved none of them. In the first stages of the battle, the Luftwaffe was able to close the straits of Dover to ordinary shipping, but at a high price. German aircrews shot down seldom got back, while Dowding recovered many of his pilots, and Beaverbrook promptly provided these with new aircraft. On August 13 the Germans began to concentrate upon southeast England and sustained such heavy losses within a week that priority was directed against the R.A.F. itself, opening the most critical period of the Battle of Britain. The vital airfields and communications centers in Kent were hammered nearly to the breaking point. Combat losses, which had favored the R.A.F., began to narrow dangerously. But on September 7, it was the Luftwaffe that broke, and turned away to bomb London. This was folly compounding defeat; the R.A.F. quickly established a more favorable loss ratio, and the London population showed no signs of demoralization under German bombing. On September 17, Hitler postponed his invasion "until further notice." In October the Luftwaffe turned to night bombing, an open admission it could no longer face the R.A.F. by day.

Night bombing would go on intensively until mid-1941, when Hitler compounded his blunders by turning to attack Russia with Britain still unbowed. London bore the brunt of night bombing; it was hit every evening from September 7 to November 3, 1940. In the winter industrial cities were heavily hit and in the spring the vital western ports. Again Hitler blundered; he should have hit these critical port facilities sooner and longer. Night bombing posed problems for both attackers (in finding vital targets) and for defenders (in finding the attacking bombers). Scientific competition was crucial in this struggle with the British having rather the better of it. Yet the damage was real enough. Four and one-half million British houses were damaged or destroyed by bombing. The House of Commons was destroyed and Buckingham Palace damaged. Many famous London landmarks were obliterated, and the working-class districts of the East End heavily bombed. Coventry, Plymouth and Hull were primary provincial targets of devastation, but despite 60,000 civilian casualties, the British war effort was never seriously impaired by bombing. Morale remained high. Churchill and the royal family were always quickly on the scene after a particularly severe raid.

But the Battle of Britain and subsequent bombing was only one part, the more obvious part, of Britain's struggle for survival. Less easily seen, but much longer and no less terrible was that grim struggle called the Battle of the Atlantic. While serious bombing ended in mid-1941, the Battle of the Atlantic did not turn decisively in Britain's favor until mid-1943, and did not really end until Germany surrendered. German U-boats had nearly stopped Britain's war effort in 1917 and came perilously close again in World War II. The fall of France and conquest of Norway provided bases that added greatly to submarine range and time at sea. German air power forced most British shipping to funnel through narrow waters into the western ports, chiefly Liverpool and Glasgow. As Britain could not use Irish ports or airfields, the task of controlling the western approaches was rendered more difficult, and effective escort range into the Atlantic was limited. Nor were there enough escort vessels. The Norwegian campaign and Dunkirk evacuation had taken a heavy toll of essential destroyers; useful escort types like corvettes were only slowly coming off the builders' ways. Although Churchill had put under way a vast escort-construction program back when he returned to the Admiralty in 1939, he did not always use these ships to best advantage. He chaffed at the apparent slowness and complexity of large merchant convoys. He wished to sail fast merchant ships independently and use escort vessels to hunt down subs. Early in the war this was literally hunting a needle in a haystack, even with asdic, or sonar to Americans, which could detect a submerged U-boat by reflections of sound waves under optimum conditions. Scientific studies showed conclusively that all but the fastest merchant ships were safer in convoy than not, and that more U-boats were sunk for energy expended by convoy escorts than by anti-sub sweeps. Churchill yielded to this evidence.

Another hindrance was lack of long-range sub-hunting aircraft, the consequence of R.A.F. long-range bombing ambitions. It required periodic War Cabinet interventions to get adequate aircraft for Coastal Command's vital anti-submarine work. Bombing attacks against U-boat facilities were largely ineffective, and thus did little to compensate. Yet the Battle of the Atlantic was won, largely through the skill of the escorts and close co-operation of aircraft as the war progressed. Most outstanding was the unflinching heroism of the merchant seamen, who received few dramatic tributes, and who repeatedly had ships sunk under them, but returned steadfastly to the task, losing over 35,000 of their mates to direct enemy action during the war.

The constant submarine menace was supplemented by occasional breakouts into the Atlantic shipping lanes of German heavy surface units. The most spectacular of these occurrences was the voyage of the German battleship *Bismarck* which in mid-May, 1941 broke into the Atlantic through the fog-shrouded Denmark Strait along the coast of Greenland. The first effort to intercept her ended in disaster when she blew the ancient British battle cruiser *Hood* out of the water. This brief action damaged *Bismarck's* fuel tanks, and oil leakage forced her to seek refuge in the port of Brest. Aircraft found her while enroute to Brest, carrier planes damaged *Bismarck's* steering gear, which allowed British heavy units to close and sink her. The fate of the *Bismarck* underscored the triumph of the airplane over the battleship, a lesson repeated for slow learners by the Japanese on December 7 and 10, 1941 at Pearl Harbor, and off the coast of Malaya, where the British capital ships *Prince of Wales* and *Repulse* were sunk.

Bombers and submarines combined to create a severe economic crisis in Britain in the winter of 1940-41 and the following spring. The western ports and the railway lines running out of them were not ready for the heavy strain put upon them; it required emergency measures to meet this crisis. Ernest Bevin, who knew dock labor at first hand, helped strongly in getting adequate organization in the ports. The railways also met the strain, through a system of inland supply depots and improved line interconnections, although it was never a very neat affair. Much coal that had come down the east coast by ship had to come in rail cars, an added burden. Late in the war when the adequate supply of coal itself became critical, young men had to be assigned by Bevin to work in the mines.

The Battle of the Atlantic, no less than the Battle of Britain, was a scientists' battle. These men invented new technical devices while skilled mathematicians analyzed complex evidence and recommended policies. At the top, Churchill had his personal scientific adviser in Professor Lindemann, who later became Lord Cherwell. He was a controversial figure because of his temperament and capacity for professional feuding, but his role was still essential. Churchill, recognizing that he had a poor grasp of the complexity of modern science, depended upon Cherwell to make these issues understandable to him so that the right decisions could be made. While the scientific record of the Churchill-Cherwell team is an imperfect one, and some poor ideas were pursued too long, the total accomplishment is still impressive.

An adjacent area of confusion was supply. The three services tended to compete against each other for supplies. Ernie Bevin jealously guarded his manpower prerogatives, which led to some spectacular clashes with Lord Beaverbrook, who was briefly Minister of Supply. Eventually this too got sorted out. Food supply was always a happier story, under the wise direction of Lord Woolton, who had a genius for making rationing palatable to the public. Public confidence in a government policy of "fair shares" was important in this. The individualistic conservative Churchill presided over the most socialist government yet in Britain's history. Public confidence was the key to British staying power in the grim, lonely months after the fall of France. No one contributed more to keeping up this confidence than Churchill himself. It was his finest hour. As the autumn storms moved up the English Channel in late 1940, it was clear that no German invasion could come for many months, and that the most critical hour had passed. Churchill's steadfast courage, and that of the British people, had reaped its just reward. Churchill now had time to turn to the awesome task of finding a way to win the war.

The military decisions of Churchill's government were largely the business of the Prime Minister and Chiefs of Staff, with the War Cabinet and its defense committees usually ratifying the decisions reached. This achieved the tight integration of political and military leadership, who worked closely together, thus avoiding the diffusion and confusion which had plagued Britain in World War I. The effectiveness of this close contact was improved by the fact that there was personal regard and respect between Churchill and the Chiefs of Staff. This did not mean there was no strain or friction.

No one who ever worked with Churchill called it a dull experience, either. Those most successful in working with Winston recognized that he was a human phenomenon, a dynamo of energy and imagination and a law unto himself, and accepted him on these terms. They were not easy terms; Churchill's working hours were unusual and he went long into the watches of the night, throwing out provocative proposals and demanding professional consideration, a heavy strain on those who worked more regular hours. A high officer wrote of one such occasion, that as he departed for bed, quite exhausted, at 3 A.M., "Winston was still listening to martial music on the gramophone!"[2] Churchill took all restraint badly, and could mutter unsoothing things about firing squads improving generals' willingness to fight. There were fears during the darkest days that the Chiefs of Staff were being overdriven. Sir John Kennedy, the Director of Military Operations, and a man of usually calm judgment, has written that "it would almost have been worth while to have two staffs: one to deal with the Prime Minister, the other with the war."[3]

Constant debate with Churchill, who used this method for hammering out agreed plans, proved too much for the highly-strung Sir John Dill, who gave way to Sir Alan Brooke as Chief of the Imperial General Staff at the end of 1941. Brooke was a tougher debater, and survived. In fact, it was not Churchill, but the Chiefs of Staff who usually won any disagreements. He would not act against their advice, however hard he pressed them. And he was ferocious in defending them from any critics. Despite his flamboyant personality, Churchill was a good administrator; a regular flow of papers channelling through Ismay and his staff regulated Churchill's direction of military policy. A similar flow ran through Sir Edward Bridges, secretary to the Cabinet, on the civilian side. There was nothing haphazard about Churchill's paperwork, which registered decisions. But it should not be confused with his famous conversations—really monologues—which served the purpose of working out ideas and working off steam. He always admitted that he made mistakes, great and small; the wonder is he made so few. In its totality his accomplishment was gigantic.

The civil side of Churchill's administration was more elaborate in structure than the military side, but equally efficient. After Chamberlain's death, Sir John Anderson, a greatly gifted civil servant, became Lord President and the committee he chaired became the chief executive agency on the civil side of affairs. Churchill left civil affairs alone except when a crisis, usually political, loomed up. Churchill's rule within his three-party coalition was that of supporting any action the war required—unpleasing to a political party or not—but getting involved in no controversial action not essential to the war. In general, given good will, this rule stood the strain remarkably well. Only once did coalition unity break, when Labour backbenchers refused to follow their leadership and voted for implementation of the Beveridge Plan of social insurance. This break did not become a breach, and the Beveridge Plan had to await the 1945 Labour government for implementation.

Churchill tended to treat these domestic crises as distractions; his chief energies were centered on finding a way to winning the war. He and Brooke were agreed that Britain could afford no more bloodbaths like the Somme and Passchendaele, and in this they were successful; British military deaths in six years of World War II were about one third of the deaths in four years of World War I. For a long time after Dunkirk the army was not an offensive force, anyway. It was gradually rearmed as a highly mobile, heavily armored force. It was not proposed to return to the continent until Hitler's empire was so undermined that the British army could deliver the final blow. The German empire was to be prepared for this ultimate downfall through a combination of economic warfare, chiefly blockade, subversion in conquered Europe, and strategic bombing. There were grievous problems with this strategy: as long as Russia was friendly to Hitler, economic warfare could achieve little. Nor was subversion very successful. Some partisans, chiefly in France and Yugoslavia, did good work late in the war, but such activities alone would never have broken Hitler's iron grip on conquered Europe. Early in the war it accomplished almost nothing. This left strategic bombing, perhaps the single most controversial issue of the war on the allied side.

Bombing advocates had long preached the doctrine that an enemy could be bombed into submission; spectacular German attacks on Warsaw and Rotterdam early in the war were used both to justify this theory and to salve those uneasy about bombing civilians. The raids on English cities, while they worked to persuade public opinion that the Germans should get the same back, also raised doubts about how much bombing alone could accomplish. Churchill always had his doubts about this, but he was determined to strike back directly at Germany. Bomber Command was the only force that could do this. But in fact, bombing technique was so bad that not many bombers came within miles of their targets. Raids had to be at night; bombers could not face the fighters by day. Late in 1941 Churchill got a report that only two-thirds of a normal bombing mission found the target and of these only one-third dropped bombs within five miles of it. As bombers were expensive, and their crews required long training, strategic bombing used up more British resources than it destroyed German resources.

In February, 1942, Sir Arthur Harris became chief of Bomber Command and determined to do better. He proposed to use area bombing, the obliteration of whole cities, to destroy German powers of resistance. While this produced great hardship in Germany, it did not cripple the German war effort. When the Americans joined the war, they tried daylight precision bombing, only to sustain catastrophic casualty rates. Harris rightly called the American bomber crews the bravest of the brave, but after a disastrous raid on Schweinfurt in late 1943, daylight bombing was suspended until adequate long-range fighter escort could be provided. In late 1944 and early 1945, with the Luftwaffe smashed, strategic bombing came into its own and destruction rained down on Germany day and night. By early 1945 the issue became rather if such devastation of German cities should continue. The destruction of Dresden at this time has particularly haunted Churchill's conduct of the war. This East German city was crowded with refugees fleeing before the Red Army, and thus the bombing took a frightful toll, the lowest estimate of which—60,000—approaches the death toll at Hiroshima. Nearly 600,000 Germans died by allied bombing in World War II. Churchill never was able to harden himself entirely to this aspect of war. On one occasion, after viewing films of a bombing raid, he asked another viewer: "Are we beasts? Are we taking this too far?"[4] Usually the most humane of men, Churchill seems to have yielded to an early desire to strike back at Germany; once begun, strategic bombing went its terrible, feckless way.

Although Churchill saw bombing as one way of hitting back at his foes, he never considered it the only way. After the fall of France, British forces were not in direct contact with German troops, but they were with the forces of Hitler's Mediterranean ally, Italy. The British position in the eastern Mediterranean rested upon Egypt, while there were large Italian forces both to the south in conquered Ethiopia and to the west in Libya. The British army commander for the Middle East, Sir Archibald Wavell, a soldier of great talents, correctly suspected that bold offensives against both Italian positions could be successful, despite large Italian numerical superiority. Wavell soon proved his suspicions, liberating Ethiopia and inflicting a humiliating defeat upon the Italians in Libya. Admiral Cunningham, the aggressive British naval commander, kept the theoretically superior Italian fleet on the defensive, carrying out a bold attack upon that fleet in Taranto harbor by carrier aircraft. Churchill for his part pushed out forces, and particularly equipment, to the Middle East all during the time when England's security from a cross-Channel invasion was by no means sure. But he also expected constant, vigorous offensive action from his Middle East commanders.

In 1941 this became no longer so easy. Hitler decided he must aid his bungling ally Mussolini, who had also managed to launch an attack upon Greece only to be thrown out promptly. In March of 1941, Yugoslavia, which had been leaning toward the Axis, suddenly reversed direction. This moved everyone to action: the British decided to risk committing an expeditionary force to Greece in hopes of creating an effective Balkan front; the troops had to come from Libya, leaving that desert front dangerously weak. In the end, everything seemed to go to pieces. German forces slashed through Yugoslavia and into Greece, where the allied front collapsed and the Royal Navy had to carry out an evacuation as difficult as Dunkirk, if not worse. In the desert, a German armored force appeared under Erwin Rommel, an aggressive and competent tactician, who promptly threw the British out of Libya. A pro-Axis revolt in Iraq threatened the British base there, and the government ordered Wavell against his judgment to send a relief expedition. He was also required to aid Gaullists in seizing Syria, where German aircraft had appeared briefly. Both these ventures were successful.

But in May, 1941, German paratroops assaulted Crete and after an epic battle secured the island. Although Cunningham had turned back an Italian fleet with heavy losses at the Battle of Cape Matapan, and executed yet another evacuation from Crete, the Royal Navy, which was taking a frightful pounding from the Luftwaffe, was stretched to the limit. So was Wavell. Churchill was distressed by the defeats in Greece, Libya and Crete, and had ordered Wavell to act in Iraq and Syria. Churchill believed that will power counted for much in war; he expected his generals to turn every post into a winning post. He wanted Wavell to attack Rommel in the desert at once. In June when Wavell unwisely yielded to Churchill's pressure, the attack was a dismal failure. Churchill, losing confidence in Wavell, sent him to command in India, from where he summoned General Auchinleck to Egypt. Auchinleck took over an immediately improved situation, for on June 22, 1941 Hitler turned away from the Mediterranean and attacked Russia. This saved the British position in the Middle East which simply had been stretched beyond its capacity.

Churchill believed any ally was better than no ally; by-gones became by-gones, and Churchill pledged all aid to the Soviets. As he put it: "If Hitler invaded Hell I would make at least a favorable reference to the Devil in the House of Commons." In an address to the nation, announcing British support for Russia, Churchill stated that he retracted none of his criticism of Communism, but that "the cause of any Russian fighting for his hearth and home is the cause of free men and free peoples in every quarter of the globe."[5]

The Russians, for their part, after sustaining initially massive defeats, rallied to hold a line when the winter of 1941 came to immobilize activity on the vast Russian front and give valuable time for bulwarking that position. The winter also brought Churchill his second great alliance partner, the United States. From the beginning of his ministry Churchill had recognized that American aid was his best chance of success; by the summer of 1941 he was convinced this aid would have to be actual American intervention in the war. Although Franklin Roosevelt, with whom Churchill had established an intimate correspondence, would give Churchill much—including vast Lend-Lease supplies when Britain could no longer pay—he would not ask Congress to declare war. Churchill arranged a personal meeting with Roosevelt at Newfoundland and came away only with a document, the Atlantic

Charter, rather than the military commitment he sought. The Japanese government resolved Churchill's dilemma by attacking Pearl Harbor. Churchill's strategic sense was sound; he went to bed the night of December 7, he has told us, and slept the sleep of the saved and thankful.

Notes to Chapter VII:

1 W. S. Churchill, *The Second World War* (Houghton Mifflin, Boston, 1948), I, 666-667.

2 Quoted in John Connell, *Auchinleck* (Cassell, London, 1959), p. 268.

3 Sir John Kennedy, *The Business of War* (Hutchinson, London, 1957), p. 173.

4 Lord Casey, *Personal Experience* (McKay, New York, 1962), p. 166.

5 W. S. Churchill, *The Second World War* (Houghton Mifflin, Boston, 1950), III, 370, 373.

CHAPTER EIGHT

Alliance Statesman: 1941—1945

On December 7, 1941 the Second World War became more truly global when Japan attacked the United States and the United Kingdom in the Pacific. Germany and Italy formally declared war upon the United States on December 11, thus essentially completing the choosing up of sides. Some time before Pearl Harbor, a Japanese statesman had told the American ambassador that history was based largely upon the operation of blind forces that cannot always be controlled in a rapidly moving world. Ambassador Grew had responded that one of the primary duties of diplomacy and statesmanship was to direct those forces into healthy channels. Churchill profoundly believed this; it was his charge against the politicians in power in the 1930s that they had not tried hard enough to do so. Accordingly he did not himself hesitate in December of 1941 to set off to spend Christmas in Washington. He correctly recognized that it was the American capital that had become the center of world affairs, and it was there the decisions would be made to shape the ultimate flow of future events.

In particular, Churchill feared that American anger over Pearl Harbor would lead to the United States concentrating her energies upon Japan first; he of course favored initial U.S. focus upon Germany, which both democracies had agreed was the greater danger as recently as the Atlantic Charter meeting. To his relief, Churchill found upon reaching the U.S. that anger had not swayed the sound strategic judgment of the American leadership. With Russia fully engaged in a struggle to the death with Hitler, and the British Empire fully extended world-wide trying to hold Japan, Italy and Germany, the decisive margin for victory belonged to the United States. No run of initial Japanese victories could obscure the fact that Japan's power in no way approached that of the nation it had so recklessly attacked at Pearl Harbor and in the Philippines.

With memories of poor allied co-ordination in World War I, Churchill wanted an agreed allied strategy for prosecuting World War II to swift victory. Churchill's first goal was effective political cooperation among the leaders of the Grand Alliance and it was he who largely supplied the cement of allied unity. Because military and political reasons alike kept Stalin in Russia, and Roosevelt's infirmity and certain aspects of the American Constitutional system combined to make travel difficult for the American President, it was Churchill who became the traveling partner of the Big Three. His correspondence, intimate with Roosevelt, more formal with Stalin, served Churchill well, but he preferred face to face conferences where he could deploy all his linguistic talents. Stalin, who required a translator, was less vulnerable to Churchill's persuasiveness than the Americans, but even he was not immune to the force of Churchill's presentations. It was Churchill himself who kept Britain an equal partner in the Grand Alliance until nearly the end of the war, long after her power had been far eclipsed by that of her two giant partners.

The Washington Conference (Arcadia) set the pattern for those that followed. Roosevelt and Churchill largely settled political matters between themselves, with aid from men like Anthony Eden and Harry Hopkins, Roosevelt's close political aide and often traveling representative. There remained the question of military cooperation. The crisis in the Pacific helped clarify this; both Americans and British were threatened by the Japanese thrust south, as were the Dutch East Indies and Australia. There a theater of operations, the American-British-Dutch-Australian (A.B.D.A.) theater, was set up. General George C. Marshall, the American Army Chief of Staff, recalling World War I confusion, believed effective command of such a theater required a single supreme allied commander, in preference to the British system of three equal air, sea, and ground commanders. Churchill yielded to Marshall's persuasion and the A.B.D.A. command was given to General Wavell, the American choice for the job.

Somebody clearly had to stand between the politicians at the top and the theater commanders in the field. This body was the Combined Chiefs of Staff (C.C.O.S.) who were the American and British chiefs sitting together during major allied conferences. Between conferences the C.C.O.S. operated from Washington, where the British chiefs were represented by a delegation led by Sir John Dill. This worked very well, as Dill got on well with General Marshall, who was the outstanding American military leader. Their close cooperation paralleled that of Churchill and Roosevelt to give to allied leadership in World War II a degree of unified control and friendly association virtually unique in history. The Arcadia Conference affirmed allied determination to defeat Hitler first, while recognizing that Japanese expansion in the Pacific must be checked as quickly as possible. Churchill had accomplished much in his American trip: an effective alliance apparatus for fighting the war and basic agreement upon the grand strategy for securing victory.

Yet victory stood far away as Churchill winged back to Britain. The initiative in the field did not yet belong to the Allies, and there was not yet agreement upon specific operations to execute their grand strategy. The United States was far from prepared to wage a world war. Pearl Harbor crippled the American battleship line; on December 10 the only British capital ships east of Suez were sunk. Churchill himself had been chiefly responsible for ordering the *Prince of Wales* and *Repulse* to Singapore, over the repeated warnings of Admiral Pound. When Pound phoned Churchill to report the loss of the two great ships, Churchill has written that "I was thankful to be alone. In all the war I never received a more direct shock."[1] He was to suffer many more shocks in the six months immediately ahead. American airplanes in the Philippines had been caught on the ground and destroyed; British air strength in Malaya was too little and soon used up. With air and sea control, Japanese armies had only to defeat isolated allied land forces. Singapore fell on February 15, 1942; its fall shook the British Empire and Churchill's government. While the British defense was poorly handled, and contrasted with the lengthy American resistance on Bataan and Corregidor in the Philippines, the island of Singapore with its large, concentrated civilian population was more vulnerable than generally recognized. This did not save Churchill from heavy attack in and out of Parliament. About this time Churchill reorganized the War Cabinet. But in fact, he changed his own war leadership not at all. The main impact of Singapore was not in Britain but in Asia. Churchill asserted that he had not become the King's First Minister to preside over the liquidation of the British Empire. But no more than King Canute could stop the tide could Churchill arrest the ebb of British power and with it, inevitably, the end of the British Empire. The surrender at Singapore, the greatest in British history, made dramatically clear to all how detached from reality the imperial dream had become.

Things seemed to be going no better for Churchill on the western desert. The intervention of the Luftwaffe in the central Mediterranean had thrown the British in Malta on the defensive. This island could no longer be used as a sally port for disrupting the flow of supplies to Rommel. Churchill wished Auchinleck to push aggressively across the desert, so that North African airfields could be gained from which to succor Malta and to protect convoys sent to resupply the beleaguered island. Most British supplies for Auchinleck himself had to go the long route around the Cape of Good Hope. In the summer of 1942 Rommel again seized the initiative, capturing the British position at Tobruk, and plunging across the Egyptian frontier toward the vital British naval base at Alexandria. But Auchinleck managed to fight Rommel, really at the end of his supply tether, to a standstill around the El Alamein position, still safely short of Alexandria. This did not save Churchill from a vote of no confidence in his war leadership, which was debated on July 1 and 2, and which he won 475-25. The great problem for Churchill's critics was to find a replacement for him. He had stood so solidly when things had looked so bad that now no one else looked suitable in his place. In fact, the worst was over; the July debate and vote rather served to throw into relief Churchill's position. He had won the hearts of Englishmen.

India was another matter. Japanese success had raised the issue of Indian nationalism. Churchill had committed some of his few reserves not to Burma as he wished, but to the defense of Malaya, under heavy pressure from the Australian government, which insisted anything else would be a betrayal of the dominion by the British. These forces were swallowed up in the debacle at Singapore, and Burma was then lost to the Japanese. A precarious defense was established upon the Indian border. In fact this marked Japan's high tide; although carrier forces penetrated into the Indian Ocean in April 1942 and sank some important vessels, the Japanese were turned back in air combat over Ceylon. The Japanese carriers were recalled to the Pacific, where they went to their doom at the hands of the U.S. Navy in May and June in the decisive battles of Coral Sea and Midway. These actions were boldly followed up by an American landing on the island of Guadalcanal in the Solomon Islands, which barred the door to Australia and gave to the Allies the initiative in the Pacific.

But Indian nationalism, once stirred, was not easily settled. The American government, strongly anti-colonial, pressed Churchill to deal generously with the Indian nationalists. Churchill took Roosevelt's views upon India no better than he had taken Baldwin's. The British Raj (rule) in India was part of Churchill's romantic view of empire, a view that had become progressively detached from actual sentiment in that empire. In March Sir Stafford Cripps, a left-wing socialist member of Churchill's government who was on friendly terms with the Indian Congress leadership, was sent to negotiate. The discussions failed. The element of timing was important. Congress wished immediate self-government and an Indian minister of defense; independence at war's end was Cripps' best offer. This was spurned by Gandhi as a post-dated check upon a crashing bank. The talks collapsed on April 10 and passive disobedience was again undertaken. The British acted firmly; Gandhi and Nehru spent the rest of the war in jail in what Churchill called commodious internment.

Elsewhere things continued to go stubbornly wrong. American entry into the war had brought initial setbacks in the Atlantic as well as in the Pacific. The U.S. Navy proved slow to learn the need for convoying, despite the British experience, and losses to subs in the western Atlantic and Caribbean were severe in early 1942. Another heavy drain on shipping was the need to supply Russia, this being virtually the only positive support the two western Allies could give their eastern partner. At first the only supply route was by convoy north along the long coast of Norway, east past the North Cape, and on to the Russian port of Murmansk. Such convoys were dreadfully exposed to weather, and to a concentration of German aircraft, subs and surface vessels. The Admiralty bluntly told Churchill that the odds were so bad that every convoy that sailed for Murmansk carried with it the seeds of catastrophe. Luck ran out for convoy P.Q. 17 in June, when confusion over the intention of German heavy ships led the Admiralty to withdraw the convoy escort and to order the merchant ships to disperse. Subs and aircraft then disposed of 23 of the 34 defenseless vessels. An order temporarily suspending the convoys brought harsh criticism from Stalin down upon poor Churchill, who faced the wrath of his own naval staff every time he sent a convoy. It was fortunate Churchill was so long schooled in adversity; he bore his full share in World War II with great resiliance and remarkably little complaint.

The American naval victories in the Pacific in May and June of 1942 announced the beginning of the turn of the tide and the offensive passed to the Allies. At the Arcadia Conference the policy of Germany first had not been accompanied by an agreed strategy against Hitler's Europe. General Marshall led American opinion in seeking a classic Napoleonic strategy: massing decisive force at the central point and smashing the enemy. The Americans had launched a vast program of military training and armament to give them the tools to achieve this goal. To them a straight-line strategy of concentrating forces in Britain and then striking directly across the Channel on to the great west-European plain and straight on to Berlin had the great appeal of economy and efficient employment of force. Churchill had many objections to the American approach, several of which were shared by Brooke. Neither man had forgotten the harrowing escape of the B.E.F. at Dunkirk, and Churchill certainly had not forgotten four bleeding years of stalemate in World War I. Churchill did not want to assault Hitler at his strongest; rather he and Brooke wished to wear down and use up Hitler's resources, both manpower and matériel. To Churchill, this meant concentrating on knocking Italy out of the war, while

Brooke wished to get the Mediterranean open to save on shipping. The long run of misfortune on the North African desert intensified Churchill's pugnacious desire to settle that affair once and for all.

To American strategists, the British interest in a Mediterranean strategy constituted a diversion from the main task of ending the war swiftly. But Churchill doubted that the largely inexperienced American army was ready yet to take on the Wehrmacht; the British army had plenty of such experience, little of it very happy. There ensued throughout early 1942 a transatlantic pushing and pulling match over strategy; Churchill traveled again to Washington, Marshall went to London; neither convinced the other. Two factors decided the debate in Churchill's favor. Roosevelt's own military experience was naval; he feared an Axis-dominated French northwest Africa as a potential threat to America. And he also wished American forces committed to fighting Germans somewhere by the end of 1942. The task of arresting Japanese progress in the Pacific and initial slowness in American production reduced the forces available for Europe. By mid-1942 the British could make a convincing case that the resources existed to invade French northwest Africa, but not Europe. By mid-year the third ally also weighed into the strategic debate. Molotov came west; he wanted to know when Russia's allies were going to begin fighting. Roosevelt gave him a promise of a second front against Germany in 1942. The British would not go this far, but did sign a treaty with Russia. As the chief politicians all now agreed on invading North Africa, Marshall gave way. His trusted subordinate, General Dwight Eisenhower, was named supreme allied commander for the operation, code-named Torch. Eisenhower was a good choice. He combined firmness of strategic purpose with strict fairness in commanding multi-national forces, and he quickly gained the confidence of the British.

As plans went forward for the invasion of French northwest Africa, Churchill and Brooke set out for Cairo and Moscow. Churchill had two goals: to find out on the scene what was wrong with the British army in Egypt, and then to go on to break the news to Stalin that there would be no new front in Europe in 1942. In Cairo from August 4 to 10, Churchill and Brooke decided upon a change of command, giving over-all responsibility in the Middle East to General Sir Harold Alexander, and command of the Eighth Army in the desert to General Sir Bernard Law Montgomery. The Americans had also shipped out to Egypt, following the fall of Tobruk, several hundred of their newest tanks, a great improvement upon the British equipment there. Both the new commanders were able men who had done well in the retreat to Dunkirk. Leaving the Middle East reinforced and in good hands, Churchill flew on to Moscow.

It was a freezing reception that Churchill met in the Kremlin when he told Stalin that there would be no second European front in 1942. However, Churchill's force of personality made its mark in persuading Stalin that his ally was sincere; Churchill revealed the coming North African landings, dwelling upon allied bombing of German cities, evidently much to Stalin's satisfaction. A thaw set in; perhaps Churchill committed himself privately to a second European front in 1943; he believed this could be done although Marshall had warned that the Mediterranean strategy would make this impossible. Churchill returned to England confident for the future. His confidence was at last rewarded. On October 23 Montgomery opened the epic battle of El Alamein and by November 4 Rommel was in full flight. On November 8, allied forces landed in French Africa. Although the landings were all successful, confusion with French authorities there followed. Those French supposed to aid the Allies could not deliver the goods; Admiral Darlan, a man tarred by collaboration, could and Eisenhower dealt with him. The so-called Darlan deal enabled the swift securing of Morocco and Algeria, and Eisenhower pushed on for Tunis. Weather and terrain, and Hitler's strong response, combined to stop the allied advance on the Tunisian frontier for the winter. Meanwhile, Montgomery was shoving Rommel back into Tunisia from the other direction. Soon there were 250,000 Axis troops trapped there. December closed with Darlan's assassination, which opened the door to some sort of progressive French government in Africa. Churchill's strategy had reaped its dividends. In January, 1943, he set out for Casablanca to explore with Roosevelt the next step in that strategy.

When the two western Allies met at Casablanca, it was clear that they were in possession of the strategic initiative; the Axis forces in Tunisia were doomed and the Russians were in the final stages of annihilating the German Sixth Army at Stalingrad. To avoid the bitter consequences of World War I, when armistice led eventually to many Germans denying their defeat, Roosevelt and Churchill proclaimed a policy of unconditional surrender. As the road to victory would lead through a restored France, strenuous efforts were made at Casablanca to form a unified French body to represent that nation's interests and aspirations. General de Gaulle claimed to be singly that body. Churchill saw the general as France's best hope; Roosevelt saw him as a potential autocrat. Much maneuvering at Casablanca led eventually to the formation of a French Committee of National Liberation that de Gaulle came to dominate, which Churchill rather expected and the Americans rather deplored. Churchill's judgment was sound here; while de Gaulle was autocratic he was not despotic, and he would be instrumental in restoring French democracy.

A positive strategic policy in the west proved hard to get. The efforts to clear the seas of U-boats and the strategic bombing of Germany were reaffirmed as alliance priorities. What to do with the armies was more difficult. Churchill's 1942 enthusiasm to cross the Channel in 1943 had quite evaporated by Casablanca. Marshall did not believe the resources for such an operation could be concentrated in Britain in time. So it was decided to go ahead in the Mediterranean after Tunisia was cleared. Not until early May, 1943 was this done. By then the strategic priorities stated at Casablanca seemed stuck. The air offensive against Germany, while consuming vast allied resources, was doing poorly. Yet more critical, shipping was threatening to become the bottleneck to the entire allied effort. Over a thousand merchant ships had been lost in the Atlantic in 1942. The first half of 1943 exceeded the 1942 rate of loss. It appeared Britain might face a food crisis. In May Churchill returned to Washington for a conference appropriately code-named Trident, to thrash out the shipping problems. Priorities were reassessed and the adequate supply of Britain reassured. Soon after this the tide turned in the Atlantic struggle; July of 1943 saw shipping losses drop sharply while U-boats destroyed rose. By mid-1943 Britain's place in the Alliance was also beginning to change. Churchill had gone practically a beggar to the Trident conference, his protestations notwithstanding. In 1943 the Americans supplied over a quarter of the British Empire's munitions. Inevitably, Churchill's ability to direct the flow of events yielded to American power.

Churchill continued to press for the strategic initiative in the Mediterranean. Events there had largely gone forward under their own momentum in 1943. The Allies invaded Sicily in July and pushed on into Italy in early September. Mussolini had fallen from power in the aftermath of the Sicilian invasion. Simultaneously with the allied landings in Italy the new Italian government announced it had surrendered to the Allies. Churchill wanted a full campaign to secure Italy up to Rome, if not further north, but determined German resistance stalled the allied advance a little north of Naples. By now an angry Stalin made clear he did not accept an Italian campaign as an adequate substitute for a cross-Channel invasion. The Americans were also convinced that such an invasion would yield greater strategic dividends than would continued Mediterranean campaigning.

Churchill had yielded to the will of his allies at the Quadrant Conference, held at Quebec in August, 1943. He was violently unhappy. He had pushed an occupation of Rhodes in the eastern Mediterranean, employing only British forces, which proved insufficient for the job. The Americans believed Churchill had become reckless in his Mediterranean ambitions, and that he perhaps harbored desires of building a British Empire at its eastern end, and refused aid. Rhodes had to be abandoned, to Churchill's chagrin.

The Mediterranean campaign, and particularly Churchill's motive in it, stirred much controversy at the time and subsequently. Critics have charged Churchill with pursuing an imperial master-plan but there is precious little contemporary evidence for this imputation. Much about the Mediterranean campaign was inevitable. The British were there—at Gibraltar, at Malta, and in Egypt—where their forces had to face Mussolini's African ambitions. Conflict was certain to occur. The allied shipping shortage cried out for getting the Mediterranean open. It was Roosevelt who decided that American troops would first see combat in the west in North Africa. Indeed, given the resources available, this was the most productive operation possible, and much was gained. A year after the North African landings, all Axis forces on that continent were defeated, Sicily was captured, southern Italy occupied and Mussolini deposed, and the Mediterranean open to allied shipping. It was only after the middle of 1943 that the Mediterranean campaign began to plague allied planning. Churchill's continued interest in operations there was not shared by the Americans, or by all his own military advisers. It is hard to define the exact character of that interest. Briefly, in late 1944, when relations with his Soviet ally hit a low point, Churchill seems to have considered an operation at the head of the Adriatic and into Austria and Hungary, to forestall the Russians. But this was only a passing consideration, and Churchill did not pursue it. The Americans steadfastly concentrated on western European operations.

The Quadrant Conference at Quebec confirmed a May 1944 date for the cross-Channel assault. Churchill now appeared to dread this coming event. He had not given up the strategic struggle when he went off in late November to meet Roosevelt at Cairo, along with the Chinese dictator, Chiang Kai-shek, to plan eastern strategy. From Cairo, Churchill and Roosevelt would go on to Teheran to meet Stalin, bringing the Big Three at last face-to-face.

Teheran revealed that power within the Grand Alliance belonged to Churchill's two giant partners. Stalin bluntly demanded Churchill's personal pledge of support for the cross-Channel invasion; this he gave, to Soviet and American satisfaction. On the other hand, Churchill successfully killed an ambitious amphibious operation in south east Asia that Roosevelt had promised Chiang. The landing craft thus saved were used to carry out a landing at Anzio, near Rome, in late January, 1944 and then the landing craft left the Mediterranean for Britain. Anzio was almost Churchill's last throw of the dice in that region. He lost. Violent German reaction penned in the Anzio force; the Italian front was thus not broken open. Bitter fighting in difficult terrain went on until Rome fell to the Allies on June 4, 1944.

Two days later, allied troops waded ashore and parachuted out of the air upon Normandy. Churchill had proved loyal to his allies in bringing this great operation into successful execution. He had been willing to take his great strategic antagonist, General Marshall, as supreme allied commander for the operation and promised to make his way smooth during the preparations for the Normandy landings. When Roosevelt decided to keep Marshall in Washington, Churchill happily accepted General Eisenhower in the top command. Early land operations were assigned to General Montgomery. Churchill supported the two generals in their demand that the initial landings be much enlarged. When Eisenhower insisted that he exercise command over the strategic air forces during the critical period preparatory to the landings and during the initial lodgment upon the continent, the air commanders balked furiously. Churchill was ready to intervene personally to resolve the conflict, but the military men got together, largely on Eisenhower's terms.

As the date for the landings approached, Churchill's enthusiasm mounted. Finally, he announced to the horrified Eisenhower that he would himself accompany the landing expedition. Eisenhower had to enlist the assistance of George VI to keep the sixty-nine year old Prime Minister off the assault beaches. If he could not have this, Churchill proposed to get as close as possible, moving down toward the embarkation ports in a special train, not without some dislocation to the government. Anthony Eden complained that the train had only one phone and one bath, and that Ismay was always on the phone and Churchill always in the bath. At the last minute, an angry Charles de Gaulle, feeling slighted in the landing arrangements, arrived to announce his intention not to cooperate. This produced a titanic outburst from an aroused Churchill. Although de Gaulle had just grounds for complaint, his threat of non-cooperation enraged the Prime Minister, who bore his own grievances without quitting. Churchill vehemently announced that if forced to choose between continental allies and the United States, he would choose the Americans every time, much to de Gaulle's unhappiness, and that of Eden and Bevin, who were witnesses, as well. Yet this last-minute crisis was also overcome, and on D-day all went well. A cheerful Churchill was on French soil a few days later.

Initial success gave way to hard slogging against bitter German resistance in the difficult Normandy countryside. Meanwhile, German V-1 weapons (jet-propelled bombs) continued to fall on London from launching pads in northern France. In late July the allied forces broke out into open country and secured a victory around Falaise which smashed German resistance in France. Montgomery raced north, with the American General Bradley on his right flank, while the aggressive American armored commander, George Patton, headed east. Partisans rose in Paris, which was liberated in late August. De Gaulle had made good his right to lead France beyond effective challenge, either from Washington politicians or French Communists, by this point. Still, controversy continued over the conduct of the campaign. The Americans insisted upon carrying out a secondary invasion in southern France on August 15; Churchill had wished this operation cancelled and its forces used in Italy. Although he manifested his displeasure upon having to yield to the Americans by code-naming the operation Dragoon, Churchill was nonetheless present to witness the successful landings.

In the autumn, the operational debate shifted north and east. Montgomery and Patton each believed he could push through crumbling German defenses, possibly to end the war in 1944, if given absolute priority upon supplies. Eisenhower believed his two field commanders were underrating German powers of resistance and overestimating how far allied logistics would stretch. Nonetheless he authorized Montgomery to attempt a bold airborne operation in the Netherlands to open a corridor through the German defenses. In late September this thrust failed at Arnhem; Patton was similarly checked as German resistance hardened all along the line.

Eisenhower then turned to the job of catching up his logistics to his advanced forces, and ordered Montgomery to open the port of Antwerp, crucial to allied supply needs. Fanatical German resistance in the Scheldt estuary area delayed this into the winter. Brooke and Churchill were disappointed that Eisenhower had not found a way to end the war in 1944. However, when in late December the Germans launched a desperate counter-attack, chiefly upon the American forces, in the "Battle of the Bulge," Churchill rallied behind Eisenhower. By mid-January the hopeless German adventure was over and the front restored. During the battle, Eisenhower had turned over command of all forces north of the German salient to Montgomery, who incautiously left the impression at a press conference that he had rescued his bungling American allies. This pushed the Americans, increasingly unhappy with Monty, past the boiling point. Again Churchill loyally intervened, and in Parliament made clear that it was the Americans who took the majority of the casualties, and he called the Battle of the Bulge a great American victory. Eisenhower, for his part, kept firm control upon the strategic situation, and upon his occasionally rambunctious field commanders, Montgomery and Patton. In the spring the supreme allied commander launched his thrusts into Germany along a broad front. American forces crossed the Rhine over an intact bridge at Remagen in early March, and at the end of the month Montgomery crossed the Rhine to the north and began to encircle the Ruhr. In early April allied forces in Italy reached the Po valley, while Patton pushed his armored spearheads into central Germany.

On the verge of victory, on April 12, Franklin Roosevelt died. A deeply-moved Churchill commemorated him as Britain's greatest friend in her hour of need. Churchill's own generous sentiment was not entirely shared by all his compatriots, distressed by increasing American domination of the western partnership. While Churchill tenaciously fought to protect Britain's interests in that partnership, he typically did not allow small or petty emotions to cloud his generous sentiments. He gave his friendship to his allies as well as his best energies to making the Grand Alliance a success.

That Alliance was showing dangerous signs of developing East-West fissure in its hour of triumph. Despite his efforts to strangle the Bolshevik regime at its birth, Churchill had embraced Stalin as an ally in the dark days of 1941. He and Roosevelt had subsequently labored to cooperate with their Soviet partner in the prosecution of the war, and the magnificent courage of the Russian resistance to Hitler's invading forces had aroused widespread admiration in the West. But the western leaders, especially the Americans, had remained cautious about reaching long-term political agreements with Russia. In particular, Stalin's repeated border and territorial claims embarrassed his western allies, who wished to postpone decisions to the end-of-war settlement. By 1944, as the Red Army began to sweep out of mother Russia and into eastern Europe, the wisdom of western stalling tactics became open to serious questions; the hazards of war might well deliver all of eastern Europe into Stalin's hands and, once he was in possession, there was really very little his western allies could do or say about it.

Within eastern Europe, the most sensitive issue to the alliance partners was the fate of Poland. Centuries old Russo-Polish hostility had flared dramatically in 1939. Out of the ruins of that most recent Polish partition had emerged an exile government, nourished in Britain, and an underground army in Poland, concentrated in Warsaw. Russo-Polish relations were worsened by German discovery of the bodies of Polish officers in the Katyn Forest. The Polish exile government blamed the Soviets for the extermination of these men; it seems most likely the Poles were correct in so doing.

In this unhappy condition matters rested when in the summer of 1944 the Red Army advanced into Poland, up to the eastern banks of the Vistula. At this point, on August 1, the underground army rose against the Germans in Warsaw, the Poles hoping that by participating in their own liberation they might secure a voice in determining their own fate. But the Red Army, halting its advance, waited on the banks of the Vistula while a terrible struggle raged through the streets of Warsaw, ending after sixty days in the annihilation of the Polish resistance. A horrified Churchill had bombarded Stalin with pleas for action, pleas that were turned curtly aside. Moscow, describing the Warsaw Poles as "adventurers," supported the so-called Lublin committee of pro-Soviet Poles as the group that should speak for Poland.

Warsaw's fate filled Churchill with foreboding, but not yet with despair. He was determined to try to get some sort of a commitment from Stalin regarding the fate of eastern Europe, and he flew to Moscow in mid-October, 1944 for grim sessions with Stalin. The Russian dictator held all the strong cards in the deck. The Red Army was already occupying Rumania, Bulgaria and eastern Poland. Churchill could only agree to Russian predominance in the first two countries, while he argued for East-West balance in Yugoslavia. He yielded to Russian predominance in Hungary, but got western superiority in Greece. Churchill has written of this agreement that they "were only dealing with immediate war-time arrangements. All larger questions were reserved on both sides for what we then hoped would be a peace table when the war was won."[2] This really only ratified the realities of the military situation, but Churchill was determined at least to keep an expansionist Russia out of the Mediterranean basin, and he meant to secure Greece from the Communist grasp. As Communist guerrillas had other plans, Churchill had to send British troops into Greece in late 1944 to support the exile government that had returned there upon German evacuation. The guerillas attacked the government and British in Athens in early December and, while Churchill was able to reinforce the military position, the political situation was a mess. So on Christmas Day, 1944, Churchill himself arrived in Athens to seek a political solution. He found an acceptable Greek leader in Archbishop Damaskinos, who was able to bring peace to Greece with British support. Stalin had notably withheld his support from the Communist guerrillas; this action encouraged Churchill to believe he could yet deal with the Soviet dictator. Indeed, the harshest criticism of Churchill came from the United States, where his intervention in Greece was viewed as an act of imperialism. Churchill was deeply distressed, for he realized that his ability to hold Stalin to his agreements, and to restrain Soviet ambition, rested in large measure upon American strength. Churchill now wished Eisenhower's spring offensive of 1945 to push as far east in Europe as possible, irrespective of the lines of occupation zones in Germany already worked out with the Soviets. There were some heated exchanges as Eisenhower avoided getting involved in

Churchill's political concerns, and the Prime Minister's appeals to Washington were unavailing. The American government held to the position that the Western Allies could not gain anything substantial by themselves disregarding their alliance agreements.

Churchill had himself thrown all his energies into getting agreements when the Big Three met at Yalta in February, 1945. The central issues in these negotiations were the post-war fate of Poland and Germany. Neither issue was successfully resolved. The western bargaining position on Poland was fatally weak: the Red Army held possession. Accordingly, the Western Allies largely yielded to the Soviet position concerning Poland's borders, which in the case of the eastern border, at least, was well-founded demographically. The best western hope for Poland's future at Yalta was a Soviet promise of free elections there. This hope would in time be bitterly disappointed as the West came to learn the Soviet definition of free elections. The western position on Germany was far stronger as their forces would soon be firmly lodged there, although not as far to the east as Churchill would come to wish. Although as recently as September, 1944, Churchill had been prepared to approve the so-called Morgenthau Plan to pastoralize Germany, the Prime Minister quickly shrank away from such considerations. At Yalta he fought hard to mitigate the Soviet terms that threatened to leave Germany a fragmented wasteland. Churchill was particularly concerned about being able to feed the population of the western occupation zones and, with memories of the Versailles settlement, did not want another settlement that western opinion would come to view as unjust. The Russians, who had recently endured savage German occupation of their own territory, were understandably less concerned for the Germans' welfare. All issues of German partition were left unresolved; de facto partition would emerge in time along the East-West occupation boundary line. This was not foreseen at Yalta.

Perhaps the greatest western failing at Yalta was not that the U.S. and Britain did not do better in the negotiations—they got about what the realities of power allowed them—but rather that neither Churchill nor the Americans were entirely forthright in telling their own publics about the difficulties of doing business with the Soviets. When this finally became evident, public disappointment would react violently, and upon the American government in particular. Yalta expanded the gap of misunderstanding and mistrust between East and West; Russia had suffered terribly from German invasion in two World Wars, and Stalin came away from Yalta bitter that his two allies would not agree to a settlement that would destroy German power forever. The last Big Three meeting, at Potsdam after Germany's surrender, only witnessed a hardening of the lines evident at Yalta. Harry Truman, the new American President, took badly Russian harshness in negotiating, and inclined toward Churchill's attitude of firm dealing with the Soviet Union. Churchill, for his part, virtually embraced Truman's information of a successful Atomic Bomb test, believing the weapon could serve to restrain Soviet ambition. Atomic Bombs first fell in August upon the Japanese cities of Hiroshima and Nagasaki to induce Japanese surrender.

By the time of those events Churchill was out of office, having been replaced at the Potsdam conference table by Clement Attlee, the Labour victor in the 1945 general election. Churchill had never had much influence upon the war against Japan, which the Americans had dominated, and when surrender came in the Pacific on August 14, eight days after Hiroshima and five days after Nagasaki, Churchill greeted it as Leader of His Majesty's Opposition. He supported the establishment of the United Nations at this time in hope that it might succeed where the League of Nations had failed.

He had led Britain through its finest hour, but also its last hour among the ranks of the great powers. Britain had expended its total energies in World War II, and by 1945 the safekeeping of the world, for better or worse, had passed to Churchill's two allies. If they had learned something about the problems and responsibilities and burdens of world power by that date, they owed a good part of that instruction to Churchill. He had ever struggled to preserve his nation and its empire, but he did not struggle any less to secure a decent life, free from terror, for all men.

Notes to Chapter VIII:

1 W. S. Churchill, *The Second World War,* (Houghton Mifflin, Boston, 1950), III, 620.

2 *Ibid.,* VI, 227.

CHAPTER NINE

World Statesman: 1945—1965

The general election of 1945 fell as a heavy blow upon Churchill. By the provisions of the Parliament Act of 1911 an election had been due in 1940, but the parties agreed to postpone the election until Germany was defeated. Churchill strongly believed in the right of the electorate to be consulted, but as the date of Germany's defeat approached, his enthusiasm for an election waned. In truth, Churchill was better cast as a national leader than as a party leader. Moreover, he had grown attached to his coalition government, one of the strongest in British history. Accordingly, he proposed that the coalition carry on until Japan's defeat. The Labour Party rejected this, so the election date was finally set for July 5. The ballot-boxes would not be opened until July 26, so that servicemen's votes could be counted. Churchill was careful that those who had done the fighting should be heard in the voting. On May 23, Churchill dissolved the great coalition and formed a Conservative caretaker government while the election campaign went on. The night of May 28, Churchill entertained the members of the coalition—Conservative, Labour, Liberal, and non-party—at 10 Downing Street and with tears running down his face told them that "The light of history will shine on all your helmets."

Churchill then plunged with gusto into what he once enthusiastically described as "the asperity and rancour of politics." He made a triumphal tour of the provinces, and was greeted everywhere by cheering crowds, whom Churchill unwisely assumed would also vote for him. But they did not. Labour had a clear program, stressing social needs, particularly adequate health care and decent housing. Churchill favored these things, too, but also cautioned against high hopes when Britain would emerge from World War II so poor. Thus the public had more confidence that Labour would deliver the desired programs. Nor had older voters forgotten the homes fit for heroes that Lloyd George had failed to build after 1918, or the high inter-war unemployment about which Stanley Baldwin had said the government could do nothing. These ghosts returned to haunt Churchill in the 1945 election.

Winston contributed generously to his own defeat by his conduct of the campaign. Always a fighter, and urged on by the equally pugnacious Beaverbrook, Churchill assailed Labour, even charging they would set up some sort of Gestapo in Britain. This extravagance, so typical of Winston, played into Attlee's hands, who could skillfully call upon the electorate to distinguish between Churchill the national leader and Churchill the party leader. The Labour leaders, themselves popular, had proved their fitness to govern by their distinguished service in Churchill's own coalition. Yet Winston's charges, although extravagant, were not insincere. He truly dreaded the leveling bureaucratization and regimentation that he believed would be part of a Socialist State. He also believed that some of the Labour leaders, like Cripps, gained satisfaction in taking the fun out of life. Nor did the asperity of politics prevent Churchill from taking Attlee with him to the Potsdam Conference, so the Labour leader could pick up the threads of discussion at once if he should become Prime Minister.

He did. The two men returned to London for the ballot counting of July 26. The results gave Labour two million more votes than the Conservatives, and 393 seats to the Tories' 213. The British people, particularly the servicemen, had voted strongly for concrete proposals of social reconstruction. Churchill was stunned, and the Americans, who knew little about British domestic politics, surprised. While Churchill was clearly hurt by an electoral rejection he took personally, his defeat was probably fortunate. Lloyd George's post-war government had been unhappy and controversial. Since Churchill did not appear to have a clear post-war program in 1945 it was probably better that he have a rest. Even Winston's great resilience was not enough to overcome the combined strains of war and age. For Churchill had gone through some strenuous bouts of pneumonia, and a mild heart attack, plus sheer exhaustion, by 1945. The years out of office would also allow Churchill time to record for posterity his account of the war years, in the six volumes of his memoirs of World War II. These memoirs were, inevitably, one man's view, but taken as a whole they have no equal in all of historical literature as a personal account of a period of crisis by one who had stood at the center of the storm.

The prolonged strain of World War II had left its mark not upon Churchill alone, but upon the whole world. It had accelerated the process of change among the relative positions of the great powers; in 1945 two nations emerged so much more powerful than the rest that they were called superpowers. Both the United States and Russia were in dynamic and expansive phases in 1945, for power politics, like nature, abhors a vacuum. Further, the concepts of political philosophy and forms of government which had developed in the Soviet Union, and which she was prepared to export to the world, were of such an order as would ensure profound distress and concern among men reared in the western liberal tradition.

Communist ideological self-confidence merged with Russian power in 1945 to present a dynamic challenge to the western states who had for centuries dominated world affairs, perhaps for too long with an uncritical assurance. Churchill had long feared the Communist threat to the values of individual freedom, which he cherished. On February 6, 1946 Stalin delivered in Moscow a forceful speech proclaiming that there could be no peaceful international world order until capitalist imperialism was destroyed. Churchill's long-accumulating concern now decisively outweighed his wartime hopes of working with Stalin to maintain a peaceful world order. The American President, Harry S. Truman, had come to much the same conclusion. Accordingly, with

Truman on the platform next to him, Churchill delivered a speech of somber warning at Fulton, Missouri on March 5, 1946. He said that from Stettin, in the Baltic, to Trieste, in the Adriatic, an iron curtain had descended across the continent of Europe, behind which human liberties were ceasing to exist. He had used such expressions earlier, but now the phrase caught the public eye, and the public did not like it. Western leaders, including Churchill, had during World War II been reluctant to reveal much of their difficulties with Stalin to the public. Their hopes of peaceful cooperation with Russia had faded rapidly in 1945 and 1946; not so the hopes of the western publics. Churchill's long anti-Bolshevik record was remembered and over 100 Labour M.P.'s put down a motion of censure against him. But practical difficulties in dealing with the Soviets in Europe seemed rapidly to reinforce Churchill's warnings. The Labour government, itself Socialist and committed to providing a minimum standard of life for all, could not avoid colliding with the anti-democratic and anti-libertarian Russian Communism.

The British government had been sending military and economic aid to Greece and Turkey, who were struggling with Communist guerrillas supported from outside their borders. The Attlee government was determined that ballots should prevail over bullets in these countries, but by early 1947 Britain was in such deep economic distress that she could send no more aid. The British appealed to Washington, which responded with the "Truman Doctrine" of supporting "free peoples who are resisting attempted subjugation by armed minorities or by outside pressures." American aid was sent to Greece and Turkey.

In May, 1947, Churchill warned that the problem was much larger. He described Europe as "a rubble heap, a charnel house, a breeding ground of pestilence and hate," concluding that unless something were done, many Europeans might embrace authoritarian Communist regimes out of sheer economic frustration and desperation even as some had embraced Hitler and Mussolini earlier. On June 5, 1947, George Marshall, now American Secretary of State, responded in his famous Harvard speech offering American aid for European efforts at recovery. Ernest Bevin, Britain's Foreign Secretary, embraced the offer, while the Soviets and their satellites rejected it. Thus western Europe alone came to profit from what became known simply as the Marshall Plan, which from 1948 to 1952 poured 12.4 billion dollars into European reconstruction, a program both generous and one of the best investments the Americans ever made. In 1947, American policy was generally defined in an influential article by the scholar-diplomat George Kennan, who advocated "firm and vigilant containment of Russian expansive tendencies," hopefully without war. Things came close in Germany; the Soviets retaliated against western steps at economic rationalization in their occupation zones by denying access to Berlin. In the winter of 1948-1949 the western powers responded with the dramatic Berlin airlift. In May, 1949 they approved a basic law or constitution for the German Federal Republic. By then, Czechoslovakia had fallen to a Communist coup, while Greece and Turkey had successfully survived such attempts. In Yugoslavia, a national Communist government had also successfully resisted Moscow's domination. On April 4, 1949 the North Atlantic Treaty Organization for mutual defense was signed by eleven countries; it was the first peacetime military alliance in the history of the American Republic. Something like stability settled over the European continent.

Britain's inability to continue aid to Greece and Turkey had underscored that she no longer ranked as a great power. Her changed status required that she reexamine the character of her relations with the rest of the world. In particular, three sets of relationships required consideration: Britain and her Empire and Commonwealth, Britain and the United States, and Britain and Europe. British participation in N.A.T.O. and Marshall Aid along with Europe directed attention to this last relationship.

On European relationships Churchill seemed more distant from the Labour government than on the subject of the Anglo-American relationship, which the government and Churchill alike treated as crucial to Britain's world position. Yet it was not always a harmonious relationship; some disagreement over just what rights Britain retained to American atomic research information from World War II arrangements led to the Attlee government carrying out its own atomic-bomb project. This was a dubious investment of limited British talent and resources. The Attlee government also showed little enthusiasm for close European ties. Ideas about European unity, which were strong on the continent, got no Labour encouragement. Britain decided to stay out of the 1950 Schuman agreements to establish a European coal and steel community. Churchill, however, seemed positively to embrace European unity. In Commons debate on the Schuman Plan he made the statement, surely remarkable coming from him, that "national sovereignty is not inviolable," and that it may be diminished "for the sake of all the men in all the lands finding their way home together." In 1949 he had attended the Council of Europe meetings in Strasbourg, where he received universal homage as the greatest living European. But while Churchill spoke encouragingly of European unity, he never exactly defined Britain's place in such a scheme of things. Rather, Britain seemed to pass endlessly around a circle of imperfectly harmonized relationships: American, European and imperial.

The British Empire gave way to the Commonwealth; British control gave way to an association of independent nations of a common English language and political heritage. The transition was most critical in India. The Labour government was determined to honor its old commitment to Indian independence; the critical issue was the Hindu-Moslem conflict. As a mutually acceptable solution could not be found, the British simply announced they would leave India and let the Hindus and Moslems forge their own solution. Lord Louis Mountbatten, a man of immense charm and political skill, was sent out as the last Viceroy to preside over the transfer of power. Faced with a crisis of time, and driven on by Mountbatten's diplomacy, the Congress Party yielded to partition. On August 15, 1947 the separate states of India and Pakistan came into being. Sadly, the largest movement for national independence in history was achieved amid terrible scenes of riot, death, and suffering as Hindus moved out of Pakistan and Moslems out of India. The whole thing was an agony to Churchill, but he had been persuaded that there was no other alternative. He greatly liked Mountbatten and Ismay, who were struggling in India. Because he respected Attlee and Bevin, he loyally refrained from adding to their burdens with extreme opposition.

The British evacuation from the Palestine mandate was even more unhappy, if such a thing were possible, than the departure from India. Hitler's slaughter of European Jewry had enflamed Zionism to a new fervor, and out of central Europe the Jewish survivors flowed as refugees toward the shining promise of a national homeland in Palestine. Arab opposition to this influx was adamant. Neither side could be restrained; no compromise was acceptable; no order could be maintained. In May, 1948 the British pulled out. A bitter war followed, won by the new Jewish state of Israel, whose existence the Arab states continued to refuse to recognize. As early as 1946 Churchill had advocated leaving the problem to the United Nations, where essentially it still remains.

The British Empire had been viable only in an equilibrium of world power that had never fully recovered from the consequences of World War I, and that the force of World War II had shattered forever. The end of empire, then, ratified Britain's demise from equal partnership in the Grand Alliance. As Churchill told Eden in 1945, there were now a great many things in the world about which Britain could do nothing. The end of an empire is never glorious, but it allowed Britain to turn to concentrate upon her domestic problems, which at war's end were in truth more than sufficient to occupy the total energies of any government.

World War II had cost Britain 300,000 military dead, and in addition some 60,000 civilians, chiefly to bombing, and about 35,000 merchant seamen, lost largely to U-boats. Of the 13 million homes in Britain, bombing destroyed a half million and significantly damaged another four million. A quarter of Britain's national wealth had been expended in the struggle, and virtually all of her overseas investments had passed into other—chiefly American—hands. This was a particularly serious matter when Britain's exports did not cover the cost of her imports. Nor could this adverse trade balance be righted by reducing imports; these had already been cut to the bone. The real consumption of all goods and services by the British people had fallen about 15 per cent during the war; there was little fat left to cut away. Heroic economic measures would be required simply to enable Britain to survive.

The Labour government that took office in 1945 was committed to the most extensive legislative program in British history. The two main categories of legislation were nationalization bills and welfare programs. Fervent Socialists long believed that nationalization of industry would be directly conducive to a more humane and equitable society. What happened, however, was that the government shouldered the burden of modernizing some outdated industries, principally coal and rail transport. These both required large doses of investment from the Treasury. The nationalized air lines also needed money in the form of an operating subsidy. Gas and electricity, also nationalized, similarly needed investment capital from the Treasury. Only the Bank of England itself, and most non-rail transport, did not immediately drain the Exchequer. The nationalized industries were run by public corporations, sometimes highly centralized as in the case of the National Coal Board, sometimes very decentralized as were the various transport boards under the British Transport Commission. But the new utopia of the old Socialists failed to arrive; so did the crypto-fascist state some conservatives had feared. The process of nationalization was not helped by the weather; a terrible winter in 1946-1947 led to coal shortages and spread disillusionment with nationalization. Only the nationalizing of the iron and steel industry created much controversy; Labour carried its act only in 1949 and the Conservatives reversed it after they returned to office in 1951.

The welfare-state legislation covered matters from housing to relief for the poor, but the most striking and controversial bill was the National Health Service Act which provided free basic medical and hospital care for all. The British Medical Association fought the proposals, despite guarantees to meet their objections, but in the end few doctors opted to stay out of the program. Like nationalization, national health service did not usher in a new utopia, but it was a vast improvement upon the previous arrangements. The chief problem here was an acute shortage of trained physicians and hospital facilities to extend adequate care to those who had largely gone without medical service prior to the Health Service legislation. No new hospital was built in Britain between 1939 and 1954, when the shortage of hospital beds was estimated at 90,000.

The real burden upon the Labour government lay in Britain's economic exhaustion in 1945. Hugh Dalton and Stafford Cripps, successively Chancellors of the Exchequer, needed more capital than Britain could generate. Canadian and American loans and Marshall Aid helped, as did devaluation of the pound in 1949. Cripps in particular labored to control inflation and thus protect the benefits of the devaluation for Britain's foreign trade. This meant a program of austerity, which could hardly be popular. Churchill led a quiet opposition in Parliament while the Conservative Party concentrated upon rebuilding its central organization and strength in the constituencies. The Labour government had probably done as well in dealing with the intractable problems of an exhausted British economy as anyone could reasonably expect, but

Crippsian austerity inevitably played into Churchill's hands, and Cripps himself was the butt of some telling Churchillian sallies.

It was a tired government that appealed to the electorate in 1950. Labour outpolled the Tories by 750,000 votes but held only 315 seats to the Conservative 298. Counting Liberals and others, the Labour margin in the Commons was only six. In June of 1950 came the Korean War, to which Britain sent troops. The cost of this, and the world inflation that accompanied it, created a new economic crisis. The government was exhausted and internally divided; the courageous and popular Foreign Secretary, Ernest Bevin, died in early 1951. Attlee decided to dissolve Parliament and in late 1951 went to the people. Although Labour outpolled the Tories by 200,000 votes, these were concentrated in heavily Labour constituencies, so that the Conservatives secured 321 seats in the new House of Commons to Labour's 295 and the Liberals' 6. A month short of his seventy-seventh birthday Churchill returned as Prime Minister to form his last government. Anthony Eden returned to the Foreign Office, while R. A. Butler became Chancellor of the Exchequer. Harold Macmillan was given the job of fulfilling the Conservative election pledge of building 300,000 homes a year. Churchill's Cabinet was small by modern standards, for he attempted to group ministries, whose heads were not in the Cabinet, under "overlords," sort of co-ordinating chief ministers. But because the overlords had no administrative apparatus or direct ministerial control, this arrangement did not work.

Churchill was supremely happy to be back in office, with many associates of his war ministry with him, but he was decidedly less vigorous now. The accumulated wear and tear of the years, and a serious stroke in August, 1949, had visibly slowed him. His Cabinet meetings, although frequent, were characteristically rambling.

He returned to office at an opportune time. In little over a year his old American friend, General Eisenhower, would become President, and end a Korean War which was winding down already. This took a good bit of strain off the world economy and allowed Britain's defense budget to be cut back. Eden was an experienced Foreign Secretary and Churchill left most of the routine work to him. An oil dispute with Iran was settled satisfactorily following a change of government there. Churchill agreed to withdraw from Egypt and the Sudan by 1954. In that year Eden was instrumental at Geneva in getting accords on Indo-China, upon the heels of a disastrous French disengagement there. The British government also restrained the Americans from intervening in that difficult situation. In April 1954, as the French were losing the battle of Dien Bien Phu, the American government proposed a joint military intervention in Indo-China. Churchill and Eden opposed this as only likely to produce an unpredictable reaction from Russia and China. Further, the British statesmen saw only a slim chance of keeping much of Indo-China out of Communist control, unless there was a massive injection of western ground troops into the region. And this they believed would be an expensive undertaking out of all proportion to the strategic value of the area.

In Europe, Britain would not merge its forces into an integrated European army but did promise to keep British divisions on the continent. This facilitated German rearmament by reassuring the French of a balanced western force without German preponderance. Churchill's last interest in foreign affairs was to seek to defuse East-West tension through summit meetings on the World War II pattern, but another stroke in 1953 stopped this initiative. Securing a peaceful world was increasingly Churchill's goal in foreign affairs in these years, particularly after development of the hydrogen bomb.

At home, Churchill left economic matters in Butler's skilled hands. For a year Butler practiced austerity, but then the improved economic scene allowed a more expansive economy. Iron and Steel were denationalized in 1953; all rationing ended in 1954. Macmillan delivered upon the pledge of 300,000 homes a year. Churchill was determined to maintain good relations with the trade unions and was successful in this. His last ministry, like Baldwin's of 1924-1929, could be called a sedate government. This did not mean that the old warrior was himself about to become sedate; he still enjoyed a good wrangle in the Commons, although he no longer sat through long debates. His elaborate, carefully prepared and highly stylized speeches were less effective in the House as they seemed too rich and dramatic for more mundane times. But he lavished his traditional loving care upon them, and he could up to 1953 still hold his own in the give and take of debates.

In his memoirs, the American Secretary of State, Dean Acheson, tells a story that skillfully depicts Churchill the politician at work. Acheson was briefly in Britain in mid-1952, when the Korean War was in stalemate. At the time the Labour opposition was pushing a motion in the Commons criticizing Churchill's support of the U.S. position in Korea. Churchill wished to react strongly in debate. Thus as Acheson returned to his London quarters at midnight, he was greeted by a bulky envelope from 10 Downing Street, which Acheson wisely did not set aside until morning. The envelope contained a speech Churchill proposed to deliver in Parliament, as a covering note explained, unless the Prime Minister heard an objection from Acheson the next morning to anything in it. A quick reading revealed that the speech referred to top-secret contingency orders given to the U.N. commander, General Ridgway. Public revelation of the orders would not be possible. So Acheson and his staff burned the night oil drafting both an objection to the proposed reference in Churchill's speech, and a substitute for it. Thus by next morning one of the American staff was at 10 Downing Street with Acheson's letter of objection. A tired Acheson went off to his day's round of meetings. He soon received word that the Prime Minister wished to see him.

The meeting at Number 10 was classically Churchillian. Acheson was shown into the cabinet room, where the old British lion sat, hunched over and alone, muttering darkly about "naked to mine enemies" and "the sword striken from my hand." When Acheson remained cheerfully unmoved by these piteous utterances, Churchill changed tack and asserted that since Acheson had effectively gutted his speech—an exaggeration of course—what did he propose Churchill should say? The Secretary of State then produced the alternative his staff had drafted, and Churchill was soon persuaded he could win the debate with it. As he showed Acheson out, Churchill asked with a sly look how had Acheson found time to do so much after receiving his midnight note. The American blandly replied: by following Churchill's own habit of working at night. The episode nicely illustrates Churchill the politician. He was master of all the arts of politics, whose little tricks he exercised with a blatant obviousness which fooled no one. He would use all his formidable skill to get his own way, but not usually at the price of dishonesty and deception.

Churchill's resilience, vigor, and humor remained remarkable in old age. He would cheerfully mutter untruths like "I have lived seventy-eight years without hearing of places like Cambodia." A list of foreign place-names would then follow, and Winston would conclude: "They have never worried me, and I haven't worried them." This cheerfulness ended abruptly in June of 1953 when Churchill suffered a severe stroke, his second in four years. While he gamely fought back, his speech was impaired and one leg remained bad. He considered resignation, but Anthony Eden, so long Churchill's heir apparant, was himself away sick. Winston rallied, so he decided to stay on. Several dates for retirement were examined and successively rejected; he did not want to go. He continued to hope he could play one last role in advancing the cause of world peace, but Churchill's active days were over. On his eightieth birthday, November 30, 1954, all Members of Parliament joined in honoring him, and he thanked them for their kindness "to a party politician who had not yet retired." Clement Attlee, his old political opponent and coalition partner, made a gracious and touching speech, and Churchill departed from the ceremony in tears. On April 5, 1955 he handed over to Eden.

Churchill remained a private member in the Commons until 1964, but age and health seldom allowed him to appear. His last speech in the House he loved came on his eighty-seventh birthday when he replied to the cheering members, "I am grateful to you all." He was a Member of Parliament for 62 years and fought about twenty elections; he held government office for nearly 30 years, twice as Prime Minister. A House of Commons man to the end, he never took a peerage as had many retired Prime Ministers. He did accept Britain's highest knightly order, the Garter, in 1953 and became Sir Winston Churchill, K.G. The same year he received the Nobel Prize for Literature.

His private years were not entirely tranquil. In 1956, his successor, Anthony Eden, became embroiled in a quarrel with Egypt over the Suez Canal, and joined with France in sending troops there during an Egyptian-Israeli crisis. Russia and the United States both reacted vehemently. The British and other forces had to be withdrawn. A sharp political crisis followed in Britain over Eden's action. In January of 1957 the ill Eden resigned. Churchill advised the Queen to send for Harold Macmillan, who quickly proved a masterful Prime Minister in rebuilding upon the ruins of his predecessor. Churchill also made a personal attempt to restore Anglo-American relations, which had been damaged by the Suez crisis.

Nor was Churchill himself left in peace. He had emerged from World War II with an immense reputation; Englishmen with warm memories of the dark days of 1940 did not stop to analyze just what the character of Churchill's contribution to victory had been. It was enough that he had "won the war." There was some shock then when criticism of Churchill's conduct of the war began to emerge in the late 1950s. The central volumes in this process were the edited diaries of Sir Alan Brooke, now Lord Alanbrooke, which appeared in 1957 and 1959. The diaries really only threw into somewhat dramatic relief what every professional soldier, British or American, in two world wars, already knew: Winston could be very stubborn about his own pet strategic ideas, some of which were not feasible and had to be rejected by the professionals. This could be a very difficult process, given Winston's rhetorical eloquence and staying-power. Dwight Eisenhower has described this process of debate with Churchill:

> He used humor and pathos with equal facility, and drew on everything from the Greek classics to Donald Duck for quotation . . . to support his position. I liked and admired him. He knew this perfectly well and never hesitated to use that knowledge to swing me to his own line of thought in any argument.

But Eisenhower also noted that Churchill never failed "to respect with meticulous care the position I occupied as the senior American officer, and, later, the Allied Commander in Europe." Nor did Churchill stop there. He provided a special London bomb-shelter for Ike when he was in Britain. "I never used or even saw the place, yet he never ceased to show great concern for my safety, although paying absolutely no attention to his own."[1] Lord Ismay, who saw Churchill nearly every day during the war, set down his impressions in a letter written, so to speak, during the heat of battle:

> You cannot judge the P.M. by ordinary standards: he is not the least like anyone that you or I have ever met. He is a mass of contradictions. He is either on the crest of the wave, or in the trough: either highly laudatory, or bitterly condemnatory: either in an angelic temper, or a hell of a rage: when he isn't fast asleep he's a volcano. There are no half-measures in his make-up. He is a child of nature with moods as variable as an April day. . . .
> I think I can lay claim to having been called every name under the

sun during the last six months—except perhaps a coward; but I know perfectly well in the midst of these storms that they mean exactly nothing, and that before the sun goes down, I shall be summoned to an intimate and delightfully friendly talk—to "make it up."[2]

Not every soldier who dealt with Churchill was as fortunate as Ismay in experiencing the Churchill sunshine following the Churchill thunderstorms, and not all were as generous as Ismay when they came to set down their recollections of dealing with Churchill. Something of a disproportionate reaction set in, as a variety of old political rivals and foes jumped into the fray with their own accounts. As the dust began to settle, Churchill's reputation showed every sign of survival. Yet Winston was hurt to think that Alanbrooke, whom he regarded warmly, had nourished such hard feelings toward him, as Churchill himself always put his daily wrangling behind him. Alanbrooke in his turn was dismayed that Churchill was hurt. It is their successful wartime relationship that deserves to be remembered. Churchill's last decade of life was not congenial for him; too much of the energy to enjoy life had been drained away by strokes. There was another in 1956 and he was very weak in his last years. A welcome death came on January 24, 1965.

The passage of time has softened but not deadened the sounds of controversy that were the steady accompaniment of Sir Winston Churchill's career. Historians now argue across the ground politicians and soldiers once fought over. To his harshest critics, Churchill was a reckless, ambitious man who sought attention, a man without abiding principles or convictions, a man who plunged headlong into disaster in one World War and who was narrowly restrained by the professionals from repeating the blunder in the second World War. His more generous critics acknowledge Churchill's generosity of spirit, his magnanimity, and his strength in adversity. But they judge him to be essentially a man of many expedients, siezing upon the proposal closest to hand, a man without any vision of the future, lacking the elements of creative statesmanship. The student of Churchill's career will want to ask to what degree the man who pursues a life in politics makes himself a prisoner of the manifold pressures exerted upon him, and to what degree he can initiate and maintain independence of action. The enquirer must ask whether Churchill was capable of rejecting superficial interests and persevering in the pursuit of creative and constructive goals. The student will find ample evidence both ways in Churchill's long and extraordinary career. Sometimes Churchill himself realized he had ambitiously pursued a goal not worth attaining. He regretted the decision to return to gold in 1925, for example.

Churchill's perception of the world and people around him was a rich and not always predictable compound of his observations, his wishes and desires, and of his powerful, romantic imagination. Lord Beaverbrook, who had known him in good times and bad, has written: "He is strictly honest and truthful to other people, down to the smallest details of his life. . . . Yet he frequently deceives himself." Beaverbrook has also testified to the autocratic side of Winston's temperament, which he called Churchill "up," in contrast to the more sympathetic person he knew in Churchill "down," the man bowed but not broken by adversity. Churchill could be imperious, even bullying. He was always more obviously interested in himself than most politicians deem wise to allow others to recognize. Both his imperiousness and egocentricity derived from his romantic sense of self-identity as a man with a rendezvous to keep with destiny. Destiny to Churchill was something noble. In 1925 at the unveiling of a memorial to the Royal Naval Division which had fought so well, and suffered so much, and had been so bound up with his own fortunes in World War I, Churchill said:

> We are often tempted to ask ourselves what have we gained by the enormous sacrifices made by those to whom this memorial is erected. But this was never the issue with those who marched away. No question of advantage presented itself to their minds. They only saw their duty to resist oppression, to protect the weak, to vindicate the profound but unwritten law of nations, to testify to truth and justice and mercy among men.

That the brave young men of the naval division saw the risks of life and death in quite these terms we may doubt. That Churchill saw them this way is beyond doubt. Churchill's zeal for life, his inexhaustible energy, guaranteed that his mistakes would be on a spectacular scale. His zest for action, and the romantic picture of life he painted for himself, could lead him into premature and unwise positions. Perhaps his defense was best put by a person who knew him well, and who said of Winston that the first time you met him you saw all his faults, and then spent the rest of your life discovering his virtues. Sir John Anderson, a civil servant of brilliant and judicious mind, believed that Winston was always strongest in office, where he could command the services of advisers to cool his ardor and urge caution against his impetuosity. Certainly, in office is where Churchill always wished to be. He was essentially a public man, and while he deeply loved his family, his private life was really only an extension of his public life. It is not enough to say that he was a public man through ambition, although his ambition was great, for his whole character supported his public life, especially through the bad times. He was best in office where his contribution to the nation could be positive and creative. Passing legislation meant more to Churchill than criticizing it; he was essentially a creative statesman. Similarly, the goals he sought were constructive and not destructive; in his early years, he conceived of the public interest more broadly than most politicians of his time. He was early concerned, for example, with women exploited in sweated trades, youngsters incarcerated in prisons, and casual laborers without jobs; he carried through positive legislation in every case. His values were profoundly humane; however, he ranked opportunity above security in his scale of values, and had difficulty realizing that while opportunity is adequate for the gifted and fortunate, both talent and good fortune are not equally distributed among men.

Churchill's strongest characteristic was his courage, both physical and moral. His physical courage needs no emphasis, but his moral courage was a more remarkable thing. In the summer of 1942, when transatlantic flights were still rare and bold adventures, his doctor noted Churchill on a flight to Washington, humming to himself: "We're here because we're here." The doctor speculated whether Winston were whistling to keep up his spirits. Throughout his life Churchill whistled to keep up his spirits through the forms of physical action. He resolved his doubts by vanquishing them. At its best, his moral courage carried Churchill through great risks to great achievements, as in 1942, when he flew long and dangerous miles to grapple personally in Egypt with the military situation there, and on to Moscow to confront Stalin with the bleak message of no second front. Churchill himself described this last task as about as cheerful as carrying ice to the North Pole. But Churchill dared not allow Stalin to doubt too deeply his allies' faithfulness, and so he went to Moscow himself. He had to make cruel decisions; he ordered convoys to Murmansk acutely conscious of the price he was demanding from the merchant seamen. In 1953, twelve years after he ordered the *Repulse* and *Prince of Wales* to what proved to be their doom, he would awake distraught from a troubled dream of that decision.

He was compassionate and humane, and suffered for his lack of tough-mindedness. For a politician he was remarkably innocent. His humanity was his deepest virtue, and when he recognized in Hitler the negation of the life-giving values of civilization, Churchill gave his full strength to upholding the forces of life against the forces of death. On September 3, 1939 he had told the House of Commons that "this is not a question of fighting for Danzig or for Poland," but rather in defense "of all that is most sacred to man. It is a war, in its inherent quality, to establish and revive the stature of man."

Churchill stands, then, foursquare in a long tradition, almost as old as man's history, that each individual is unique, and his destiny special, and that his institutions should nourish, and not strangle, his individuality and should ensure to him a large area of personal freedom. This is not a tradition that has fared well in the twentieth century. Future writers may come to judge Churchill the last giant of a vanished race of men.

Notes to Chapter IX:

1 D. D. Eisenhower, "Churchill as an Ally in War," in C. Eade, ed., *Churchill by His Contemporaries,* (Simon & Schuster, New York, 1954), pp. 159, 164.

2 Quoted in John Connell, *Auchinleck,* (Cassell, London, 1959), pp. 472-473.

Bibliographical Note

Books about Sir Winston Churchill are legion; this list is limited to those most useful and easily available to the student. An asterisk indicates a paperback edition and the date of publication given is for that edition. Some useful surveys of British history during Churchill's most active years are A. F. Havighurst, *Twentieth Century Britain* (second edition, 1966)*, W. N. Medlicott, *Contemporary England, 1914-1964* (1967), and A. J. P. Taylor, *English History, 1914-1945* (1965)*. There is a good critical bibliography in Taylor. The sources available for the history of this era are thoughtfully discussed in C. L. Mowat, *Great Britain since 1914* (1971)*. Frederick Woods has compiled *A Bibliography of the Works of Sir Winston Churchill* (second edition, 1969) which has an appendix listing books written about Churchill.

In some respects Churchill is still his own best biographer. Particularly attractive is W. S. Churchill, *My Early Life: A Roving Commission* (1958)*, originally published in 1930. Churchill's memory for details was not perfect, and his account needs to be corrected by reference to the official biography, the first two volumes of which were written by his son, Randolph S. Churchill: *Winston S. Churchill* I. *Youth* (1966), II. *The Young Statesman* (1967), which carry Churchill's career to the outbreak of World War I. Upon Randolph Churchill's death the official biography was taken up by Martin Gilbert, who has carried the story through 1916 in volume III (1971). This is the best single volume yet written about Churchill, and presents the best picture of Clementine Churchill's importance in her husband's life. There are companion document volumes to the official biography's narrative. A more critical view of Churchill's career is Robert Rhodes James, *Churchill, A Study in Failure, 1900-1939* (1970). A second volume completing Churchill's active career is planned.

Churchill's first ministerial appointment is very well told in Ronald Hyam, *Elgin and Churchill at the Colonial Office, 1905-1908* (1968). Also useful is Brian Roberts, *Churchills in Africa* (1970). Winston's own views as a Liberal can be read in *The People's Rights* (1970), originally published in 1909. An attractive view of Churchill then is by Asquith's daughter, Violet Bonham Carter, *Winston Churchill as I Knew Him* (1966). There are some interesting views of the Liberal Churchill in Lucy Masterman, *C.F.G. Masterman* (1969, reprint edition).

The most readable and dramatic account of Churchill's storm-tossed career from the outbreak of World War I to the fall of the Lloyd George coalition in 1922 is to be found in Lord Beaverbrook's trilogy: *Politicians and the War, 1914-1916* (1968, reprint ed.), *Men and Power, 1917-1918* (1968, reprint ed.), and *The Decline and Fall of Lloyd George* (1963). Beaverbrook's story should be compared to Cameron Hazlehurst, *Politicians at War* (1971) which, like Beaverbrook, centers on Lloyd George, but is also valuable for Churchill. Future volumes will carry Hazlehurst's tale beyond 1915. Churchill's relations with Beaverbrook at this time and later can be found in Kenneth Young, *Churchill and Beaverbrook* (1966).

The Dardanelles campaign has its own large literature. Two views rather critical of Churchill's role are Trumbull Higgins, *Winston Churchill and the Dardanelles* (1963) and Robert Rhodes James, *Gallipoli* (1965). These should be compared with Martin Gilbert's volume III of the official biography and Paul Guinn, *British Strategy and Politics, 1914-1918* (1965). Churchill's stewardship at the

Admiralty, 1911 to 1915, and the Dardanelles campaign are presented from a rather professional naval viewpoint in the first two volumes of Arthur J. Marder, *From the Dreadnought to Scapa Flow* (five volumes, 1961-1970). Marder has also edited the colorful correspondence of Lord Fisher in *Fear God and Dread Nought* (three volumes, 1952-1959), in which Churchill frequently appears. Churchill defended his war record in *The World Crisis* (four volumes, 1923-1927). A fifth volume, *The Aftermath* (1929) covers some of his activities in the post-war coalition government.

A survey still valuable for the inter-war period is Charles L. Mowat, *Britain Between the Wars, 1918-1940* (1955; paperback edition, 1968)*. Richard H. Ullman carefully examines Churchill's hostility to the Bolsheviks in *Britain and the Russian Civil War, November 1918-February 1920* (1968), which is volume II of his *Anglo-Soviet Relations, 1917-1921*. Churchill's role in the last crisis of the Lloyd George coalition is told by David Walder, *The Chanak Affair* (1969). Lloyd George, in his *War Memoirs* (six volumes, 1933-1936), is neither entirely flattering nor entirely fair to Churchill.

There is much about Churchill at the Treasury in Keith Middlemas and John Barnes, *Baldwin* (1970) and in Tom Jones, *Whitehall Diary, 1916-1930* (three volumes, 1969-1971), edited by Keith Middlemas. The third volume deals with Ireland. A biting critique of Churchill's economic policies is John Maynard Keynes, "The Economic Consequences of Mr. Churchill" (1925) which can be found in his *Essays in Persuasion* (1963)*. A more friendly view by a civil servant who worked for Churchill at the Treasury and later is P. J. Grigg, *Prejudice and Judgment* (1948).

Churchill's views on the movement of international affairs between the wars can be found in Arnold Wolfers' still valuable *Britain and France between Two Wars* (1966)*, first published in 1940. Neville Thompson, *The Anti-appeasers* (1971) shows Churchill's isolated political position in the late 1930s.

Our view of World War II is still dominated by Churchill's own account, *The Second World War* (six volumes, 1948-1953). A comprehensive survey of Churchill's wartime stewardship is Maxwell P. Schoenfeld, *The War Ministry of Winston Churchill* (1972). Churchill's finest hour is seen in two very different but equally valuable accounts: Sir Edward Spears, *Assignment to Catastrophe* (two volumes,

1954-1956) and Isaiah Berlin, *Mr. Churchill in 1940* (1970, reprint edition). There is an evaluation of Churchill the wartime Prime Minister and strategist in John Ehrman, *Grand Strategy* volume VI (1956). Sir Alan Brooke's diaries, rather stressing the difficulties of achieving an agreed strategy with Churchill, have been edited by Sir Arthur Bryant as *The Turn of the Tide* (1957) and *Triumph in the West* (1959). A more dispassionate evaluation of these difficulties has been set down by Brooke's subordinate, Sir John Kennedy, in *The Business of War* (1958). A positively sunny picture is painted by Lord Ismay, *Memoirs* (1960).

The story of two generals who found Churchill a hard taskmaster is told by John Connell in his *Auchinleck* (1959) and *Wavell* (two volumes, 1964-1969). Two naval views are S. W. Roskill, *The War at Sea* (four volumes, 1954-1961), which is rather critical, and Sir Peter Gretton, *Former Naval Person* (1969), which is more sympathetic, and also covers Churchill's 1911-1915 tenure at the Admiralty.

Two later Prime Ministers have left accounts of serving in Churchill's wartime government: Anthony Eden is cautiously critical in *The Reckoning* (1965) and Harold Macmillan is admiring in *The Blast of War* (1966). A rare dominion (Australian) view can be found in Lord Casey, *Personal Experience, 1939-1946* (1962). Charles de Gaulle has pronounced his verdict on Churchill in his *War Memoirs* (three volumes, 1955-1960). There are also valuable companion document volumes. Churchill's relations with his allies can be found in E. L. Woodward, *British Foreign Policy in the Second World War* (1962; an expanded five volume record is in the process of appearing, 1970-   ), W. H. McNeill, *America, Britain and Russia: Their Cooperation and Conflict, 1941-1946* (1953), and Herbert Feis, *Churchill, Roosevelt, Stalin* (1957; paperback edition, 1967)*.

R. E. Sherwood, *Roosevelt and Hopkins* (1948) fleshes out the story of Churchill's relations with the Americans from the papers of Harry Hopkins. A good account of the Atlantic Charter meeting is T. A. Wilson, *The First Summit: Roosevelt and Churchill at Placentia Bay 1941* (1969). Churchill's differences with his American allies over strategy are thrashed out in F. C. Pogue, *George C. Marshall* II: *Ordeal and Hope* (1966), and Trumbull Higgins, *Winston Churchill and the Second Front* (1957). A brief, but very capable summary is Michael Howard, *The Mediterranean Strategy in the Second World War* (1968).

Russian views of their British ally are hard to come by; the best available is *Stalin's Correspondence with Churchill and Attlee* (1965)*.

Two views of Churchill's handling of domestic politics during the war are Brian Gardner, *Churchill in his Time* (1968) and G. M. Thomson, *Vote of Censure* (1967). Their views should be compared with the picture of Churchill which emerges from Harold Nicolson's superb *Diaries and Letters, 1939-1945* (1967), the middle volume of three edited by Nigel Nicolson.

Wartime scientific controversies can be followed in C. P. Snow, *Science and Government* (1959) which is critical and a bit melodramatic, and in the carefully researched Lord Birkenhead, *The Professor and the Prime Minister* (1961). An official treatment of the strategic bombing controversy is Sir Charles Webster and Noble Frankland, *The Strategic Air Offensive against Germany* (four volumes, 1961); an unofficial view is A. Verrier, *Bomber Offensive* (1969).

A book that created a controversy is Lord Moran, *Winston Churchill. The Struggle for Survival, 1940-1965* (1966). Responses to some of Moran's views can be found in Sir John Wheeler-Bennett, editor, *Action This Day* (1969). Anthony Storr has written a psychoanalytic view of Churchill which can be found in A. J. P. Taylor, editor, *Churchill Revised* (1969), which contains several valuable essays.

There is relatively little available on Churchill's career after 1945. Attractive views of Churchill the elder statesman are given by Harold Macmillan, *Tides of Fortune, 1945-1955* (1969) and Dean Acheson, *Present at the Creation* (1969). J. D. Hoffman, *The Conservative Party in Opposition, 1945-1951* (1964) is useful, and there is something of a tentative analysis in Robert Blake, *The Conservative Party from Peel to Churchill* (1970).

Index